Egyptian Gene
of the Nephilim

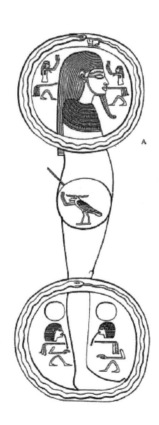

Acknowledgments
With thanks to David Parry and the Nephilim Anthropology Conference for the invitation to explore this theme.

Contents

1. First Word 5

Hieroglyph 6

The Bull of Ombos goes astray 6

2. The Bible Story 15

Lilit 18

Giants 20

Miniaturization 22

The Flood 22

Egyptian sources 23

Apophis 24

The Fallen 25

Richat 26

Names 28

Demons 31

Manetho, and the survivors 32

Plato's Atlantis 33

The Pillars of Seth 34

3. The Sphinx Enigma 35

The Red Sea Scrolls 40

4. Abydos & the Giant 43

The Osireion Giant 47

5. The Seriadic Land 51

The Old Chronicle 55

The Horoi 57

The House of Life 60

6. The Submerged Ones 62

The Shebtiw & the Battle at the Beginning of Time 63
More on the Shebtiw 76
Decay and resurrection of the island 79

7. Egyptian Star Maps 80

8. The Problem of Evil 87
Female Shebtiw? 94

9. The Underworld of the Soul 100
The Osireion 100
Becoming a Giant 104
The Giant and the Dwarf 106
Request for a dream oracle of Besa 111

10. The Apet and the Ancestors under the Floor 113
11. Conclusion 118

Appendix: The Horoi 119
Select Bibliography 120
Index 127

1. First Word

Beresheet, the first word of the Bible means 'In the beginning'. Thus begins the foundation myth of the ancient Hebrews, including the account of their long sojourn in the land of the ancient Egyptians. The earliest parts of this narrative are full of strange things, including, famously, and very early on, a terse mention of the Nephilim, a class of supernatural entities, who erupt into the text only to disappear again almost as soon as they appear. But appearing briefly as they do, at the beginning of the long Genesis story, serves, in my opinion, to make them all the more significant. Here is the text:

Genesis

6:1 And it came to pass, when men began to multiply on the face of the ground, and daughters were born unto them,

6:2 that the sons of God saw the daughters of men that they were fair; and they took them wives of all that they chose.

6:3 And Jehovah said, My spirit shall not strive with man forever, for that he also is flesh: yet shall his days be a hundred and twenty years.

6:4 The Nephilim were in the (land) earth in those days, and also after that, when the sons of God came unto the daughters of men, and they bare children to them: the same were the mighty men that were of old, the men of renown." Bible, American Standard Version.

The American Standard translation of this passage says the Nephilim were "In the earth", which seems a bit awkward, and sounds as if they are somehow underground, a point seized upon by some *Hollow Earth* theorists. The confusion is dispersed by a consultation of the original Hebrew, which I did with the assistance of Miryamdevi, who points out that the same term is used a line or two later for humans, (Ha-adam), who are also in what must in fact be the *land* (Aretz) rather than the *Earth*.

It was always assumed that this part of the myth originated somewhere within the Mesopotamian myth cycles, either from Sumerian or Babylon. No-one had, as far as I know, been asked, as I was, to explore if it might have some sort of basis in Egyptian mythology.

So this was where I started, with what seemed to be the Elephant in the room: could the Nephilim and the events that surround them, have any resonance in Egypt? And, much to my surprise, I found an Egyptian equivalent of the Nephilim. Deep mythology is what I call those very old stories that have no real home but seem global and part of the consciousness of all humanity. And as is often the case with comparative and deep mythology, one tradition illuminates many others.

Hieroglyph

What about the word *Nephilim* itself, does it exist in Egyptian hieroglyphics? Linguistically, *Nephilim*, is a word of Semitic or Asiatic origin, which is a group of languages that include Hebrew, Arabic and Egyptian. There is an Egyptian root Nefy-im - meaning those who have gone off course, thus applied to various wrongdoers. The determinative, a special sign appended to a word to help distinguish between words with a similar sound, to help clarify its meaning. A *determinative* is unspoken, silent, element like this bull with halter round its neck (E1 in the standard sign list). The halter might be the way these animals are brought back from where they do not belong. Where has it been, perhaps spreading its seed where it should not have done! Which come to think of it is one of the things the Bull of Ombos, otherwise known as Seth does, when he tries to have sex with Hathor the cow.

The Bull of Ombos goes astray

Once upon a time
The Seed Goddess Hathor (*t3 mtwt*)
Took a bath on the shore in order to purify herself in the oasis
Seth was out walking and he saw her
He saw her jewel encrusted girdle, he saw her bare ass,
And it turned him on
Then he mounted her as a ram mounts a ewe
He covered her as a bull covers a cow
But for the seed goddess it was all wrong
And she went straight to his head
To the region between his eyebrows where the full moon sits
And he lay down, exhausted on his bed
and was stricken with the seed become poison

⌐ ⌐ nf wrong, wrong-doing, Leb. 129; L. to D. II, 6 (⌐ ⌐ ⌐); m nf 'wrongfully', GAS ⌐ ⌐ ⌐ nfy wrongfully, van. ⌐ ⌐ ⌐, ⌐ ⌐, L. to D. II, 6, n.

Then his other wife Nephthys (Anath),
The victorious goddess
An androgynous woman who acts like a warrior
Who wears a man's kilt
Tied with a woman's sash
Distressed, went to her father the Sun god Ra
He said "what is the matter with you"
Nephthys, victorious goddess
Androgynous woman who acts like a warrior
Who wears a man's kilt
Tied with a woman's sash
I am near to my evening setting
I know you want me to cure Set of the effects of
his overstrenous coupling with Hathor
The poison of the bad seed out of place
Let Set's stupidity be a lesson for him
Hathor, the seed goddess was destined
for the bed of the sun god above
He will make love to her with his heavenly fire
His will be as hard as steel when he enters her.

Hearing this the divine Isis said:
I am the Nubian woman
I have come down from heaven
I have come to realise the seed in the body
of every mother's son and every mother's
daughter
And cause them to return in good health

For as Horus lives
So shall all live:

As it happens, the Nephilim were also sometimes envisioned as Cattle. In one passage of *The Book of Enoch* (Charles & Dillman edition, chapter 86) one reads:

"And again I saw with mine eyes as I slept, and I saw the heaven above, and behold a star fell from heaven, and it arose and ate and pastured amongst those oxen. And after that I saw the large and the black oxen, and behold they all changed their stalls and pastures and their cattle, and began to live with each other. And again I saw in the vision, and looked towards the heaven, and behold I saw many stars descend and cast themselves down from heaven to that first star, and they became bulls amongst those cattle and pastured with them [amongst them]. And I looked at them and saw, and behold they all let out their privy members, like horses, and began to cover the cows of the oxen, and they all became pregnant and bore elephants, camels, and asses."

Here quite clearly are the fallen angels but envisioned as cattle, along with their earthly mates!

It all makes sense when one recalls the phenomena

known as the ancient "Cattle Cult", one of several well known manifestations of the primeval spirituality, traceable to the Stone Ages when dangerous wild cattle were first domesticated. It is sometimes said that our first gods were the animals, such as the once wild cattle, that we at first hunted then eventually domesticated, eating their beef, drinking their blood and using their skin for our clothes and tools. So it wouldn't be surprising to find all this referenced in Egyptian myths, which are some of the world's oldest recorded and where every god has a bovine avatar, including Seth. His presence is detectable in all these stories. Here's another example of that from ancient author Plutarch: (IAO40) wrote:

"Typhon of old conquered the party of Osiris. For Egypt was once sea; for which cause many places in the mines and in the mountains are found to contain shells to the present day; and all springs, and wells, whereof there are many, have their water brackish and bitter; as though being a stale remnant of the former sea which had collected there. " (*Isis and Osiris* 40)

And there is some truth to this, the Egyptians noticing these relics all around them. The so-called Pyramid mountain just outside modern Luxor actually has a beach with seashells high up in the hills.

Or consider a whole geological formation at Giza called the nummulitic formations, west of the great pyramid of Khufu, or Kheops as he was known in older sources. The rock here is full of coin sized, fossilized "nummulites".

These remarkable things were noticed in antiquity where someone came up with the likely story of them being the remains of the lentil rations eaten by the Israelites, as they laboured on the construction of the pyramids. Aside from whether the Israelites did actually labour on this particular pyramid, the fossils are remarkable in other ways, as one of the largest of all single cell organisms.

Once you start looking there is loads of this material in Egypt, a land with so many wonders it would be easy to overlook. Take Wadi el Hitan which means "Valley of the Whales" in the Fayum. Fayum from an old word meaning ocean. The valley is so named for its fossilized whale skeletons, the remains of an ancient beaching of a Whale pod in what is now the desert surrounding the oasis. Whales are ancestors of the Hippopotamus, who still rove the Nile valley. Dangerous creatures who are yet another avatar, yes you guessed it, of Seth.

One of my favorite relics of the Egyptian *Nephilim* are known as the "Black Bones of Seth". These are found in the tombs at the place named by the Greeks after the, note, Giant, Antaeopolis. Antaeus a fusion of Horus and Seth. In Arabic Qau

10.0 mm

The so-called Pyramid Mountain, in whose shadow many Egyptians are entombed. Below: nummulites, fossilised remnants of what was the largest single celled organism.

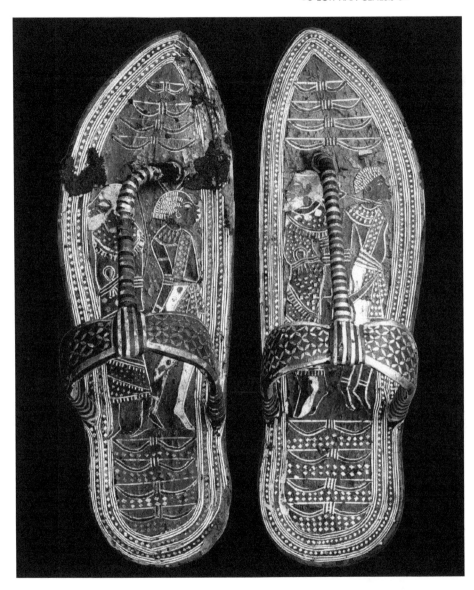

King Tutankhamun's sandals recovered from his tomb in the Valley of the Kings. The bows and enemies of Egypt crushed beneath the wearers feet. "These boots are going to walk all over you" magic in action.

el Kabir. To the native Egyptians Tjebu, Djew-Qa, meaning sandal. It is notable how all these sames through the millenia retain the same vibe. Again I remind you of the important theme in connection with the Nephilim, that of power buried in the earth.

Tjebu, or the Sandal Maker is its Egyptian name. There is a whole science to the study of town names known as Toponyms. Obscure mythological incidents are often encoded in them. By clever detective work it is deduced that the same is a reference to a failed rebellion, ie that of Seth, in which the rebels are treated to one of the arsenal of brutal punishment, to be flayed and their skin made into sandals. The magical sandals of Tutankhamun are well known for their decoration with the symbols of the enemies of Egypt, thus everyday the king walked all over them, an act of sympathetic magick.

The important thing to recall about the Black Bones of Seth mentioned above is that they are bones without skin. The skin presumably made into sandals at some unknown ancient moment. Or more likely the ancient bones found here in great numbers are connected with the fate of the Rebels, which is described as such in an inscription from the famous temple of Hathor at Dendera (See Mariette, *Denderah* IV plate 60)

The tomb shafts were actually packed with fossilized bones, which must have been an obvious and notable feature of the local geology. Nearby must be a prehistoric fossil graveyard of the ancient ancestors of the Hippo that lived and died there.

One such creature had an estimated length of 4.3 metres (14 ft), a shoulder height of 2.1 metres (6.9 ft), and a weight of 3900-4500 kg (8600-9900 lb), Hippo gorgops was larger than its living relative, H. amphibius. Another feature setting it apart from H. amphibius was the placement of its eyes. Modern hippos have eyes placed high on the skull, but H. gorgops had eyestalk-like orbits extruding above its skull, making it even easier for the creature to see its surroundings while (almost) fully under water. This species was described by German scientist Wilhelm Otto Dietrich in 1928. (Wikipedia)

Another recently discovered species, though wrongly named species, 10-foot-long (3 meters) species, dubbed Phiomicetus anubis, was a beast; When it was alive more than 43 million years ago, it both walked on land and swam in the water and had powerful jaw muscles that would have allowed it to easily chomp down on prey, such as crocodiles and small mammals, including the calves of other whale species.

What's more, the whale's skull bears a resemblance to the skull of the jackal-headed Anubis, giving it another link to the death deity, the researchers observed. "It was a successful, active

Left: Hippo Ancestor
Below: Black Bones of Seth

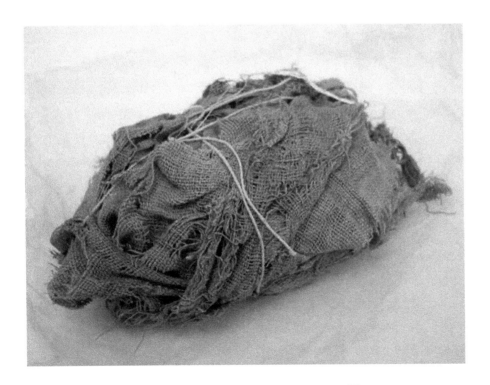

predator," study lead author Abdullah Gohar, a graduate student of vertebrate paleontology at Mansoura University in Egypt, told Live Science. "I think it was the god of death for most animals that lived alongside it." Seth fit this role much more closely than Anubis.

The locals would have been familiar with the living species of Hippo and recognised these bones as special ancestral species. Thus they collected and placed literally tons of them as backfill in the shafts. Their discovery was likely started with a sandstorm, itself a manifestation of the desert god Seth. Some strong wind rose up and blew the desert sands away, exposing a secret hidden underneath: the hard, pitch-black bones of what looked like a gigantic monster.

The Hippo, being one of the most dangerous denizens of the Nile, was considered to be an avatar or the God Seth, who together with his brother Horus was venerated here as a composite entity. No doubt this is the reason for their ritual use of these distinctive bones in the tomb defenses. Their shiny black colour gives them the appearance of iron. The earliest tombs here are from the 12th dynasty when the only iron would be from meteorites, "iron from the sky", which was considered a relic from an ancient Typhonian past.

The *companions* of Seth were also said to be giants or titans who hid in animal form. See *Book of the Dead*, seppls 18 & 134 (from Griffith)

Anubis looks out across the Theban necropolos

Antaeopolis

2. The Bible Story

Returning to the Biblical account of the Nephilim it is worth reminding ourselves of its context. The scholars of Egypt's library at Alexandria had been commissioned to make a Greek version of the Hebrew bible, for deposition there.

This narrative is found in the pseud-epigraphic Letter of Aristeas to his brother Philocrates, and is repeated by Philo of Alexandria, Josephus (in *Antiquities of the Jews*), and by later sources (including Augustine of Hippo) :-

King Ptolemy II, once gathered 72 Elders. He placed them in 72 chambers, each of them in a separate one, without revealing to them why they were summoned. He entered each one's room and said: "Write for me the Torah of Moshe, your teacher". God put it in the heart of each one to translate identically as all the others did.

Philo of Alexandria writes that the number of scholars was chosen by selecting six scholars from each of the twelve tribes of Israel. Which would concur with Jewish tradition that the legendary tribes were still in existence until the later destruction of the Second Jewish temple in Jerusalem by the Romans. The Greek translation was considered a distortion of the original sacred text and unsuitable for use in the synagogue. So its history is more important as the basis of subsequent Christian Bibles.

According to the Hellenistic Jewish scholars who made the translation, Nephilim meant great or giant: "... but also fallen, as in fell down from the upper realm, heaven, but not necessarily thrown down. They are sons of god(s), angels, who desired to take on human form, and are thus half human. Same term also applies to the offspring of their union with human women, which they initiate or are seduced, depending on the source. They have supernatural powers. Some are thought of as bad but others not so. They have knowledge of magick which they teach to humanity. Other versions say, significantly, that they also taught metalwork, astronomy and alchemy. Sometimes also known as the Gibborim or heroic ones. Elsewhere they are called "the watchers" from the use of Aramaic word Irim, which also means angels. *The Book of Enoch* is not part of the Bible though closely related, also calls them (Enoch 179n) *Watchers*. Here also reminding us that they were "Angels who fell in love with the daughters of men" Nephilim is the plural. They were not human, perhaps like other monsters, they were unable to reproduce with the interaction and sexualcontact with the fertile daughters of men. Being all male they need biological women to fulfill this imperative. This is the major reason for the contact.

We can gather a little more information about this from the most important of Kabbalistic texts, the *Zohar*, which was compiled around the 2nd century, but later rediscovered by the Knights Templar who brought the Aramaic text to medieval Spain where it was translated and published. The Zohar is an expert, esoteric commentary on the Bible.

Beresheet is the Hebrew name of the first book, and means, appropriately "The Beginning". The Christian translators rendered this as *Genesis*, when *Beginnings* would have been more appropriate, as it would then have preserved the important characteristic of the book, which may seem insignificant to those with no awareness of the grammatical mysticism at play here, B, is the second letter of the Hebrew alphabet. It being a mystery I surmise might still be discussed in Kabbalistic circles, why didn't the book begin with Aleph, as the "grammatical" mysticism would dictate? This is the first word of the first book, why not use the first letter of the alphabet?

I made good use of the online translation provided by the Kabbalah Centre where one reads the following comment on Beresheet B: Verse 423

"The Nefilim were on the earth..." (Beresheet 6:4). Rabbi Yosi taught that those CALLED NEFILIM were Aza and Azael and as we have learned, they were so called because the Holy One, blessed be He, dropped (Heb. hepil) them from the upper sanctity. How, you may well ask, can they subsist in this world? Rabbi Chiya said that they are among those referred to as "Birds which fly upon the earth" (Beresheet 1:20). And these, as we have discussed, appear to men in the form OF HUMAN BEINGS. And how, you may ask, do they transform themselves FROM THE SHAPE OF AN ANGEL TO THAT OF HUMAN BEINGS? As we have learned, they can transform themselves into all kinds OF SHAPES, and when they come down INTO THIS WORLD, they clothe themselves with the garments of earth's atmosphere and take on human form."

Later same Zohar there is more detail: Beresheet B: Verse 424.

"Aza and Azael, who rebelled above, and whom the Holy One, blessed be He, caused to fall from heaven, were forced to put on and to live with the garments of the earth. They could not divest themselves of these garments AND COULD NOT RETURN TO THEIR FORMER RESIDENCE WITH THE REST OF THE ANGELS. THEY REMAINED FOREVER ON EARTH. Subsequently, they were seduced by earthly women. They exist to this day, teaching sorcery to people. They begot sons, whom they called 'mighty' and 'giants.' The Nefilim are referred to as "sons of Elohim," as has already been explained." *Zohar* (online version from Kabbalah Centre)

The Zohar here offers a possible explanation or speculation as to how the non-human Nephilim were able to have commerce with the diminutive humans. It's either a problem or something that invites ridicule, how can two such different species interact sexually? The solution is that one of them has to change stature. It sounds like some sort of permanent shapeshift to something closer in form. A similar speculation accompanies the cinematic reboot of *Superman*, how could he and His love Lois Lane have sex, wouldn't his winged seed also be superstrong, and burst forth from her body?

The ancients' solution was to say that this transformation, if it happened at all, would only be possible one way, there was no going back. In the *Superman* saga, he renounces his superpowers and is only then able to have a human relationship with Lois. In both cases the transformation is not so thorough that some aspect of the alien "DNA" remains entangled with that of regular humans.

Later, when the existence of this class of intermediate humans is taken as self-evident, it is put to work to solve other existential problems. Thus within the later Rabbinical tradition, the Nephilim are used as an explanation for the existence of a class of beings we call demons. It could be that the existence of this intermediate class was not something that was really a part of the oldest strata of Jewish thought. In a nutshell, there were no demons in ancient accounts. It seems to have become more of a thing after the period of captivity in ancient Babylon in the 7th century BCE, and thus one would expect it to be dominated by Persian notions. The Jews returned to Jerusalem, changed by the many new ideas they had encountered.

"In Babylonia the Jews came under the influence of both the Chaldean and the Persian belief in good and in evil spirits, and this dualistic system became a dominant factor of Jewish demonology and Angelology." (https://www.jewishencyclopedia.com/articles/5085-demonology)

Lilit

In the Zohar a link is made between the mother of all demons, the sisters Na'amah and Lilit, and the Nephilim:

Acharei Mot: Verse 360

After THE DEMONS were born to Adam, he had daughters from these spirits that were similar in beauty to those on high and those below. Therefore, it is written, "The sons of Elohim saw that the daughters of men were fair" (Beresheet 6:2). All were going astray after them. There was one male, who was born to the spirit from the aspect of Cain, and he was named Tuval Cain. A female was born with him. People were going astray after her, and she was called Na'amah. From her came other spirits and demons. They were hovering in the air, revealing matters to the others who were below, IN THE WORLD.

These children, NAMELY DEMONS AND SPIRITS, that she bore to humans are SEEN IN DREAMS to human females who conceive from them and bear spirits. They go to the primordial Lilit and she rears them. She goes out into the world, seeks children, sees human male children and attaches herself to them in order to kill them. Then she joins with the spirits of the children and goes with that spirit. Three holy spirits come. They fly before her, take from her that spirit, place it before the Holy one, blessed be He. There they study before Him.

If anything, their ideas seem closer to those of the Egyptians, who, like many cultures, had no generic word for "demon". Etymologically, the Greek derived term "daemon" or "demon" means divider or alloter, and from Homer's time onwards, an operator of unexpected & intrusive events in a person's life. Unlike Olympian gods, *daemon* was an impersonal thing, unpredictable, anonymous & often frightful in manifestation. Thus it was connected with fate. (*Oxford Dictionary of the Classical World*). Plato, perhaps influenced by Egyptian and Hindu thought, added a new concept of the "guardian daemon" that accompanied a person in life, & postmortem, acted as a judge or advocate. Contemporary magical practitioners often describe a spiritual entity known as the Holy Guardian Angel, that is attached or comes into existence at birth or conception.

Later in a classical world dominated by Greek philosophy, the demon became an idea nobody could ignore. So how did the post exile Jews square all this with Biblical creation? The answer was by expanding the notion of the Nephilim.

Thus it seems a terse Biblical account was worked on, fleshed out in what scholars called "second temple Judaism". The knowledge of this comes mostly from the famous Dead Sea Scrolls, which belonged to the library of Qumran, the citadel of the Jewish Essene sect. They seem to have been specialists on demons and how to deal with them. These people were influenced by or perhaps composed the *Book of Enoch*, ht*he* first and considered to be the most notable work of apocalyptic literature outside of the Biblical canon. It is ascribed to the great grandfather of Noah, who is of the Sethite line, therefore it is more of this lost knowledge from before the flood. With some exceptions the book is not considered canonical although it was obviously well known and respected by Jews in the classical world.

In it we learn that there were unexpected consequences of the earlier illicit intercourse between angels and humans. The Angels paid a heavy price for this lapse, according to *The Book of Enoch*, a special place in Hell was reserved for the guilty, chained until the end of days, when they would be destroyed in a final cataclysm.

Their offspring were viewed as an intermediate class of beings. If we accept this idea then it may contradict the idea that some living people possess Nephilim DNA or rather "blood", perhaps the so-called "witchblood". The line of reasoning in the *Book of Enoch* would be that the offspring, though themselves Nephilim are an intermediate class of beings, occupying as they do, the realm between humans and the gods.

This idea of a third synthetic class of being, found in many nearby cultures, including the pharaonic, in whose "anthropology" we can recognises three classes of being: the living, the dead, and the Gods, which when translated makes the neat Egyptian phrase viz: "Ankhew, Akhew, & Neterew".

Thus the Jewish Encyclopedia (online) gives the example of the "ben nefilim," which became the demon of epilepsy, and "Ruach Zecharit," the spirit of nightmare (Bek. 44b; Tosef., Bek. v.3; Schorr, in "He-Chaluz," 1869, p. (15).

Prof Gideon Bohak, who wrote the entry on demons in the *Encyclopedia of the Bible*, has an informative lecture available on Youtube in which his says that the Hebrew word for Bastard, "Mumzere", is what the Essenes called the offspring of the union between the son of heaven and children of men.

The *Book of Enoch* again tells us: "Gabriel said to the Lord: 'Proceed against the bastards and the reprobates, and against the children of fornication: and destroy [the children of fornication and] the children of the Watchers from amongst men [and cause them to go forth]: send them one against the other that they may destroy each other in battle: for length of days shall they not have." (1 Enoch X.9)

This becomes the origin of the demons. Professor Bohak also says, these beings are, from a human point of view, far more accommodating, that is to say, useful to us. More useful that is than the Angels, who are powerful but apart from their singular function as messengers, are aloof and mostly unaccommodating.

Hence Enoch (1 VIII) remembers that "Semjâzâ taught enchantments, and root-cuttings, Armârôs the resolving of enchantments, Barâqîjâl, (taught) astrology, Kôkabêl the constellations, Ezêqêêl the knowledge of the clouds, Araqiêl the signs of the earth, Shamsiêl the signs of the sun, and Sariêl the course of the moon."

The Egyptian alchemist Zosimus quotes a passage from *Book of Enoch* saying they also taught metallurgy, for which the Jews of his times were famed, and is the basis of Alchemy, the colouring of metals. (Grimes, *Thesis on Zosimus*, 2010)

So all these strange and alien ideas have iterations outside of the Hebrew tradition, going back to a common mythic root, in Egypt, to which the Israelites trace their own origins. The second book of the Bible, is known as Shemot, the Book of Names ("These are the names of the sons of Israel"), and is called Exodus by Christians. It contains the well known narrative of Abraham, Jacob, Joseph and Moses *et al.*

Just as demonology is an international tradition, so too is the ancient memory of a catastrophic flood, which was supposed to eradicate all the illegitimate, the "non-kosher", that had crept into creation; to wipe the slate clean. One major symptom of a defective nature would be the existence of Giants.

Giants

The Enochian account expands the terse Biblical verses and gives the giants a size, three thousand ells (1 Enoch VII.2) which is about 1500 meters, which seems preposterously high and we can only suppose to be a symbolic number, like 40 days and nights, though in this case the meaning is lost in the mists of time.

Some commentators have in the past objected to the idea of "Giants", perhaps because it seems silly. The main controversy seems to be, from a Christian point of view, that this seems to undermine the idea of a singular all powerful god. If you believe in one god, then reading all this, one can't help asking, who are these other beings?

I think one can take this seriously and accept that this is what the ancient authors really did have in mind. It is a "true myth" or "memory" thought important enough to record. From a magical point of view, the notion of becoming a giant or of assuming a giant persona is regarded as at the very least, a powerful psychological technique, which has been called "giant" consciousness. You might encounter this notion of assuming a superhuman persona in many diverse mythologies and assume if you dig deep enough, you will find it everywhere. So what does it mean?

One example I like is found in magical invocation when the magician "assumes the godform". This rather grand expression means that they imagine themselves in an heroic form, which usually means as larger than life, could even be gigantic in stature. This is an imaginative process that can produce real and important psychological change. It also works in the opposite direction as in reducing something in stature, a process often reserved for troublesome or dangerous entities, which are usually envisioned at less than life size, sometimes ridiculously so, as in the illustration of the god Horus spearing a diminutive image of the dangerous entity Seth.

The Egyptians wrote the playbook on this game of giant versus diminutive. It is a technique that we continue to use in mundane situations, for example where one finds another person troublesome or oppressive, one makes them feel small etc, certainly in one's view of them, perhaps even in the way you interact. This can be therapeutic. I could easily multiply the examples of its psycho-magical use in

Giant Horus spearing diminuitive Hippo from Edfu, Egypt

21

real life. In such a visualization it can be easier to imagine your opponent as getting smaller than you getting bigger or gigantic. But the upshot would be that you are, in effect, a giant.

Almost all cultures have some manifestations of this Giant/Little people dialectic, and this gives us a possible meaning, for all those tales of Giants and Fairies, found in much of the world's folklore. The author Jan Fries writes about something similar in his exploration of Celtic and Northern traditions. Jason Read comments: "I've yet to find a culture where there isn't a primordial giant. I think the vision of the cosmos as a giant entity is universal and common to the earliest shamanic visions. Look at the folk reflection even in Jack and the (cosmic axis) beanstalk" From that we might say it goes with the territory of shamanic exploration, that this almost always involves some encounter with what we might call Giant consciousness.

Miniaturization

For the corollary we might consider how "Jonathan Z. Smith has observed that one of the most striking features of the corpus of Greek magical papyri is the 'miniaturization' of temple rituals which have been adapted for use in a domestic context or in the repertoire of a mobile professional."

This comes right up to date in contemporary Chaos magick where improvisation is also a form of miniaturization. I'm thinking also so-called "kitchen" & "freeform" magick, all can be related to the changes of scale from the ancient techniques

One of the oldest rituals known to us from the Pyramid texts, is that of "Opening the Mouth", performed on a statue, to bring it to life or activate it. It comes as no surprise that this same ritual survived in various iterations of decreasing scale. It was miniaturized. For more on this see Moyer, Ian, and Jacco Dieleman. "Miniaturization and the Opening of The Mouth in a Greek Magical Text (Pgm Xii.270-350)." *Journal of Ancient Near Eastern Religions* 3.1 (2003): 47–72. Web.

The Flood

Returning to the Biblical motif, we can also say that wrapped up in all this, is a memory of a vast flood or perhaps we should say *The Flood*. Such a catastrophe at the beginning of history, or just before it restarted, was an event remembered everywhere, including, as we shall discover, in the Egyptian records.

Jewish sources also tell us that the existence of the giants was what prompted the creator to send the flood, it was his attempt as the supreme deity to correct things by eradicating those whose existence was deemed to be a mistake. One example comes from *The Book of Jubilees*, an ancient Jewish text, another of those not considered canonical, other than by Ethiopian Jews, but is perhaps all the more interesting because of it. *Jubilees* (7:21–25) states that ridding the Earth of these Nephilim was one of God's purposes for flooding the Earth in Noah's time. This work is also notable for describing the Nephilim as *evil* giants.

Various dates are given for this flood, in all cases it is envisioned as an event coming before history as we know it started. This reminds me of the famous book *The End of History*, which seemed so relevant, perhaps the idea of *Before History* is equally as important a concept.

The flood was the prelude to history, and was what happened before any written accounts were possible. Later texts give a date for the flood, Anno mundi 2242, i.e. years from creation of the world and Adam. From the beginning to the time of Enoch, was said to be 1282 years. There is some sort of mystical numbers game at work here, one whose rule book is currently lost to us, perhaps it is Kabbalistic.

All these dates seem to place the flood somewhere in what we would call the Neolithic age, literally New Stone Age, the final centuries of a great age of stone, which was both an end and a beginning for humanity as we know it. It could be when stable agriculture was established and the historic age began, all was predicated on the development of writing systems. It was inevitable that those Neolithic people would come to record their memories and beliefs in words rather than just pictures.

However, despite God supposedly hitting the *reset* button, the Nephilim survived in some form, perhaps because they were giants. But as we know, many other species did not. It was what we call a great extinction.

Egyptian sources

There are several important Egyptian sources where we can find parallels to the Nephilim myth of the Bible. Most were also well known to the learned Jewish Rabbis, who, as we mentioned earlier, were set to work as translators of the Hebrew Bible into Greek. They certainly would have known the works of Manetho, an Egyptian priest whose name means "Beloved of Neith". Neith is an ancient goddess whose temple in the Delta was the place where many ancient travellers were told some very strange stories concerning events long ago. Although a native Egyptian, Manetho wrote in Greek, the elite language of his time, which was the 2nd century BCE.

I already mentioned the accounts of ancient catastrophic floods. Egypt, if only by reason of longevity, has some of the best records of such deep history. Furthermore, it has some very ancient accounts that describe a mysterious group of giants known as the *Shebtiw*. Their name actually means the

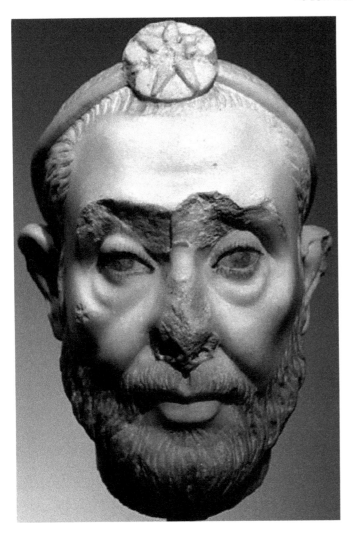

Manetho "Beloved of Neith", Egyptian priestly author in Greek of a history of Egypt

"submerged ones", something we can explore in further detail later on.

Apophis

Another record from this time is to be found in the famous temple at Esna in Upper Egypt, dedicated principally to Khnum. He was the source of the Nile, and a creator, using its clay and water. Alongside the alchemical Khnum is the ancient "mother" Neith and Heka, personification of magick. From there scholars have translated the following extraordinary inscription:

> "...I will destroy everything that I have created. The earth will return to the Nun, to the water, as in the primordial age. I am the one who will remain with Osiris, I'll turn back into a snake, which is not known by men and is not seen by the gods."

Also know from the *Book of the Dead* and the *Coffin Texts*

This Esna inscription dates from the late Roman era in Egypt but it was obviously still current, preserving as it does, memories from Egypt's earliest philosophy. Never has the phrase "the writing is on the wall" been more apposite. Whoever executed the temple decoration in this period, presumably the scribes (the Shesh), was well aware that the pharaonic culture was drawing to its close, and thus with some urgency made use of these last temple commissions, as a means to memorialise many important myths from Egypt's distant past, before it was too late. It is a literary phenomenon we encounter time and time again in late Egyptian monuments.

This particular text from Esna is all the more extraordinary because it also tells us the original or hidden form taken by the creator god, that of a giant serpent. This is the colossal serpent, which played a major role in Egyptian creation and indeed destruction. One might ask, are they extinct?

This serpent could easily be one of those Nephilim, who both created the primordial Egyptian world and who then trampled it down again.

And indeed, as we expect of the Nephilim, they knew magick, which they used in the above tasks. It is safe to assume that one of their number was Egypt's deadly serpent of "non-being" known as Apep or Apophis. She or he, has been called "the mother of curses" in the sense that a great deal of Egyptian magick came into existence to fight her, thus we can call her the demonic mother or catalyst. You could say she taught magick because a great many counterspells were designed to fight her. These form another group of spells with a long history, still going strong.

Apophis is often discussed together with a god with many supposed similarities, known in later times as Typhon, meaning the one "who causes the flood". In the truly Egyptian tradition, this indigenous god was called Seth, (Set in older accounts). He is the only one of the gods who is able to resist Apophis, because he can stare her chaos in the face and not be afraid. Her "evil eye" does not phase him, and unlike his contemporaries, he is not paralyzed with fear.

The Fallen

Thinking again of the Hebrew accounts where the literal meaning of Nephilim is from Hebrew *nafal* - to fall, it was only by later embellishment that it acquired an additional meaning of *Giant*. Some modern commentators find this meaning is not legitimate. They say the only thing we can say is that these entities have fallen or somehow dropped from the upper sanctuary, that is from heaven. Nothing else is really known for certain.

Nevertheless, elsewhere in the Bible the same word is used to describe Goliath, the Philistine champion, meaning really that he was large and strong, though not in any superhuman or gigantic sense. In that narrative, before invading the land that was to become Israel, spies were dispatched to scout out the situation. Most of them returned with reports that were very discouraging in this regard. Whatever, the original sense of *giant* was, according to some scholars, actually read backwards onto the earlier accounts. To make something fortean of this is not, according to this interpretation, a valid conclusion.

Others, such as expert Jaap Doedens (2019 : 291-294) say that these accounts are definitely describing something more than mighty humans, and this accords with the classical view of for instance a sect of gnostic Sethites, to whom the Nephilim were not human but supernatural entities. The giants of the so-called Vulgate version of the Bible, really does mean that. And part of the ancient evidence for them would be the mysterious megalithic structures and dolmens, which so often must have appeared the work of superhuman powers.

The Sethites were the supposed descendants of Seth, son of Adam. In ancient anthropology, they were considered a "short lived race" rivaled by the Cainites, the descendents of another of Adams' sons, Cain, who famously killed his brother Abel. After Noah, the Sethites (which supposedly became all of surviving humanity) and divided into three separate groups, the Hamites, Semites, and Japethites, each named after Ham, Shem and Japheth; the three sons of Noah respectively (*Bible Wiki*).

The name was revived by members of a gnostic sect, who claimed an affinity with the original Sethites. In origin they were a Jewish group, of possibly priestly lineage, a mix of the so-called Barbeloites, named after *Barbelo*, the first emanation of the Highest God, and a group of Biblical exegetes, the Sethites, the "seed of Seth." It has to be said that the name Seth has a number of interesting homonyms, most famously the Egyptian aboriginal deity Seth. Lord Seth, in some versions of his myth, also killed his brother, Osiris. In others stories he was killed by his brother Anubis, for reasons not too dissimilar to the biblical dynamic, thus the stories are thought to be related. For more on this search for the "Myth of the Two Brothers".

Richat

I'm going to digress here to mention an interesting phenomenon, to be found not so far away from all these events, this is the so-called Richat Structure in Mauritania. This rather extraordinary geological phenomenon is entirely natural but even in prehistory, from the earliest stone ages, it attracted ancient visitors, pilgrims perhaps, who left evidence of their gatherings and industries there.

It's well known that the original people who settled in the Nile valley moved from various parts of the African subcontinent. This was truly a long time ago, maybe eight thousand years or more. The Richat is in Mauritania, in the extreme western Sahara, 2500K miles from Egypt's western desert, from where

The Richat structure, a natural phenomenon in Mauritania. Sometimes compared to plans of ancient Atlantis

the original settlers arrived. It's what's sometimes called a songline, could it be a memory of visiting the ancient structure, that was not passed down through the millenia?

The Richat Structure is the location of exceptional accumulations of Acheulean artifacts. Hand axes from about 8000K years ago, but also late Paleolithic arrowheads, it was obviously some sort of hunting ground. It also had neolithic industry sites but no dwellings, but there are playa lake deposits. No remains of human activity have been found in the innermost circle, perhaps because it is too inaccessible.

It could be that its very weirdness, its colossal concentric rings, visible from space, has all entered into many old sagas, such as the Atlantis myth. So once again, it could be a case of where even a mistaken identification can change the world.

Names

So, returning to the ancient explanation for words such as Nephilim, from a modern perspective we have a tendency to think we know more, and can correct the mistakes of ancient writers. Classical historians, mostly from the Roman epoch, regularly speculate on their own prehistory and the obscure meanings of words. One such was Plutarch, a Roman citizen but culturally Greek, who wrote what is still one of the most important accounts of the legendary history of Egyptian Gods, Osiris, Isis and Typhon. He made several attempts to explain the meaning of the names of Egyptian gods. Thus he says Seth's name really means "to overmaster" or overpower" (IAO 371). The eminent scholar TeVelde and expert on Seth reminds us to consider that Plutarch was closer to the action than we moderns can ever be, and we should not assume we know better what they meant.

So, back then, there were four theories or views about who the "Sons of God" : also called the Nephilim, who they were. One key characteristic is that they have intercourse with human beings. Ie "the daughters of men" and this gives rise to children, who are also known as Nephilim – who have a heroic nature – and large stature (*giborim*). So the Nephilim:-

1. Were they Angels (Hebrew *Malakh*). If so, they would need sufficient corporeality, they need physical bodies when they are usually seen as more ethereal, able to be messengers but not much more.

2. Sometimes, the old accounts use this same word to refer to "Mighty ones" as in the heroes of their times.

3. The Sethites, as already mentioned as the most ubiquitous of the ancient gnostic sects, or those

who leave most records, viewed the Nephilim, or their descendents, as essentially another kind of human.

4. Divine beings, gods who had intercourse with humans. This theme is said by some to be taken over from Greek Myth where the motif is common enough, e.g. Heracles, was the son of Jupiter and the mortal Alcmene. So it might be surmised this story of the Nephilim shows a lot of Greek influence.

Following from view four, one of the distinctive motifs here is that of the possibility of a relationship between supernatural entities, whether we call them gods or angels, with humans.

It seems to me that a far more obvious example of this comes from one of the very countries in which the Talmud was translated, that is to say Egypt. It would not be difficult to find many stories like this in the contemporary pharaonic and popular folk culture of the time. Just walk outside the Library of Alexandria where they worked and consider who founded the city in which it stood.

In fact the theme of intercourse between gods and humans is a fairly familiar one in Egypt. The most obvious example of this is to be found in the theory of divine kingship in Egypt, being the notion that the pharaoh is a god.

At the beginning of the New Kingdom, the *God's Wife of Amun* was a royal title held by royal women (usually the wife of the king, but sometimes by the mother of the king), when its extreme power and prestige was first evident. The New Kingdom began in 1550 BCE with the Eighteenth Dynasty. These were the rulers who drove the Hyksos out of Egypt. Their home city was Thebes, which then became the leading city in Egypt. They believed that their local deity, Amun, had guided them in their victory and the cult rose to national importance. Adjustments to the rituals and myths followed.

The title, God's Wife of Amun, "referred to the myth of the divine birth of the king, according to which his mother was impregnated by the god Amun." "If she was impregnated by the god, this implies that gods and humans do have intercourse. It is likely that for example the Greek traveler Strabo produced a garbled account of the institution in his histories of Egypt where he gave it the misleading name "sacred prostitution".

He was really thinking of the Divine Votaresses, aristocratic Egyptian women, who served as priestesses and slept in special incubation chambers, near tombs. They there communed with spirits of gods, and the dead in nocturnal rituals connected with this cult, involving dreams and visions. This also involved some private magick, when local women sought the help of the gods to start a family.

Another lively example arises when the Greeks first came to Egypt and began their own dynasty of kings. It started with Alexander the Great and his defeat of the Persians. In the peace, he visited the famous oracle at the oasis of Siwa and was told that his father was the god Amun, who had impregnated his mother in a dream. Perhaps it was well known at the time that his mother Olympias did claim something similar.

Part of the same romantic legends concerns the fate of Egypt's last native pharaoh, Nectanebo who was driven from Egypt by the conquering Persians. Legend has it he went to the Macedonian court in Greece, disguised as a soothsayer. Queen Olympias was an initiate of the Dionysian mysteries, and it was rumoured that she may have been impregnated at one of their ecstatic rites, when people became possessed by the god. Could Nectanebo have been present in these same rites?

Another important thread in Egypt is the widespread belief in what we could call *incubi* and *succubi*, demi-gods or daemons spirits that were widely feared for their propensity to visit people in their sleep and have sex with them. The Magical Papyri (PGM) are full of such rituals to counter them. One in particular is a bit of ancient storytelling in which one such famous account is recalled:

One character seems distressed by an unfortunate turn of events that we can presume he sees no solution to in magick. His confidant is unclear of the problem, which he states at the end of the passage:

" … [the sun] will stand still; and should I order the moon, it will come down; and should I wish to delay the day, the night will remain for me; and should / we in turn ask for day, the light will not depart; and should I wish to sail the sea, I do not need a ship; and should I wish to go through the air, / I will be lifted up. It is only an erotic drug that I do not find, not one that can cause, not one that can stop love. For the earth in fear of/god, does not produce one. But if anyone has it and gives it, I beg, I beseech him: "Give! I wish to drink, I wish to anoint myself."

"You say that a handsome phantom keeps appearing to your daughter, / and this seems unreasonable to you. Yet how many others have fallen in love with "unreasonable bodies".

(PGM XXXIV 1-24)

Plutarch, a Neoplatonic philosopher, had a view on what may have been a not uncommon problem in his world. He comments thus:

"... the Egyptians make a distinction here that is reckoned plausible: while a woman can be approached by a divine spirit and impregnated, there is no such thing as sexual intercourse between a man and a divinity."

An awful lot of this discourse is about women and their supposed propensity not to play the game, to have desires of their own, which the male authors often find difficult to comprehend.

Demons

All accounts seem to have difficulty deciding what is the difference between them, gods and angels? An Angel – Hebrew *malakh* usually seen as a "messenger" literally "god's worker" – Spelt Mem, Lamed, Aleph, Kaph, easily confused with Melekh or "King" spelt Mem, Lamed, Kaph. (With thanks to Diti, a native Hebrew speaker, for this insight). As in Egyptian myth, these messengers are often just "lesser" gods.

Demonology is a rich and interesting topic. In Judaism, there seems to have been some debate about demons, and how they might have come into existence in the first place. You will not find a direct explanation in the Bible proper. One has to search Gnostic texts, such as those discovered at Nag Hammadi, to learn that demons are the outcome of the intercourse between the Nephilim and humans. All of which fits with the idea of demons as intermediate beings.

Because they are in the middle, they are naturally suited as mediators between their parents' species.

Here's a relevant passage from the *Book of Enoch:*

8. And now, the giants, who are produced from the spirits and flesh, shall be called evil spirits upon the earth, and on the earth shall be their dwelling. 9. Evil spirits have proceeded from their bodies; because they are born from **men**, [and] from the holy Watchers is their beginning and primal origin; [they shall be evil spirits on earth, and] evil spirits shall they be called. 1 Enoch XV

This is a common enough view, that one finds in Coptic Christianity in the 10th century of our era. The following story comes from a collection of Coptic manuscripts is:

There once was a monk, respected and reverenced by all, until, after violating the virgin daughter of a king, says he was incited by the devil to murder her, disguising her death as natural causes. But the queen, her mother, is warned, by another devil (*epiboulos*, "The Plotter") via a dream of the real manner of her daughter's death. So in this case, the demon is actually quite helpful to people and enables them to get to the truth of a difficult situation.

Although demons have a reputation for being nasty, this is not invariably the case, and indeed it might be they have to be provoked before they lash out, usually as a result of an accident, much in the way one steps on a snake. (Crum (1905) 382-3 BM mss 919)

We often misread the language of these old texts, giving demons a great status than they in fact ever claim. We think of "Satan" with a capital S, as having some almost omniscient role. But mostly it's Satan with a small "s", or even plural, Satans, as a class of being rather than one being. This in the *Book of Enoch* is says

"And I heard the fourth voice fending off the Satans and forbidding them to come before the Lord of Spirits to accuse them who dwell on the earth." (1 Enoch XL)

Further on in the same book is more information about where the flood originated:

LIV. 7.-LV 2. *Noachic Fragment on the first World Judgement.*

7. And in those days shall punishment come from the Lord of Spirits, and he will open all the chambers of waters which are above the heavens, and of the fountains which are beneath the earth. 8. And all the waters shall be joined with the waters: that which is above the heavens is the masculine, and the water which is beneath the earth is the feminine. 9. And they shall destroy all who dwell on the earth and those who dwell under the ends of the heaven. 10. And **when** they have recognized their unrighteousness which they have wrought on the earth, then by these shall they perish.

As I was writing this I had many useful dreams, the incubation of which has become the way I do my own magick :– The thing about their size is that it is about being effective, what the Egyptians termed *akh*. About hitting the mark, which they show me in a strange way, by the image of throwing chickens into the temple or the strange object we find there or take from someone's house. A small ceramic thing which we can drink from, but then produces a rather strange phenomenon, a sound perhaps, which makes us nervous at the enormity of the potential we have unleashed.

Manetho, and the survivors

So did the Nephilim live on as the Egyptian gods? I'm sure that is how the Egyptians would have seen it. Moreover, everyone who wrote about this in the ancient world, being avid readers, were always aware of their contemporaries views. Manetho is a prime example of an ancient writer whose work was crucial in this regard. Other ancient Egyptian writers of his time linked his theories with the Biblical account of "Watchers" or "Egregori". This was just another name for the Nephilim hence :

> Eusenbius wrote with good reason, criticizing the Egyptians for their foolish talk; and in my opinion, Panadorus – an Egyptian monk writing on chronology, circa 395-408 is said to be wrong in finding fault with Eusebius here, on the grounds that Eusebius failed to explain the meaning etc etc (p11 Waddell)

In the Bible, Egypt was called Mizraim, after the grandson of Noah (Genesis 10) who ruled after the flood. It is still, but the name Mizraim is actually Egyptian in origin, being the dual form "the two lands", the ancient name for Egypt. Egypt's first king sometimes called Naracho (Waddell 2004 : 23) The name continues in modern Arabic *Misri* – Egyptian. Sometimes these non-biblical accounts say that three races lived in Egypt, the Aeritae, the Mestreaei and the Egyptians but these names are variations of the same word Misri or Mizraim. It all goes to show these names remain relatively unchanged over the millenia.

Manetho, the Egyptian priest whose name, depending how you break it down or parse it could mean "Truth of Thoth"), or more likely, given his connections "Beloved of Neith" was from a place in the Egyptian delta called Sebennytos, modern Samannud. Its population then was mixed Greek & native Egyptian. It was obviously a bit of an intellectual hotspot. Hundreds of years before this it was visited by Solon, from whom Plato claimed to have learned the story of Atlantis, in which we also encounter giant beings, much like the Nephilim.

Plato's Atlantis

Manetho's history, the *Egyptiaca* was written for Ptolemy II, *the very* same pharaoh who commissioned the Greek translation of the Talmud mentioned earlier. Manetho's book tells the story of Egypt's kings going way back to a "nameless" aeon, that is before the more familiar lists of kings or pharaohs usually considered to be historical. Most scholarly commentators do not know what to make of this very "deep" theory, and mostly ignore it as an oddity. They confine themselves to looking at what he says about those considered the historical lists of kings. The game is to try to reconcile what he says with the discoveries of archeology and Egyptology.

Manetho also described the generations of gods, humans and angels before the great flood, which all records in the region say happened, though they might disagree on dates, and whether it happened more than once. His book, is in three parts, corresponding to the rule of the Gods, the Demigods and the Spirits of the Dead, and then the mortal kings who ruled Egypt down to the time of Darius, King of the Persians" (Eusebius in Waddell 2003 : 3)

The original book *The Egyptiaca*, did not survive but was so popular at the time, and so important a source, that summaries, so called *epitomes*, which were remodeled or rewritten by hellenistic Jews "in such a way that the Jewish chronology became compatible with that of Manetho" (Wadell : xix). This remodeled version was then used by Roman-Jewish author Josephus and in turn from him by early Christian authors. Thus are ideas passed around.

The Jews of the time were "naturally, keenly interested in this history because they felt a strong connection to those they viewed as their ancestors from the time when they lived in Egypt, the famous patriarchs of the Bible viz: Abraham, Joseph and Moses, the leader of the Exodus. Later Jewish scholars were keen to base their theories on the origin and antiquity of the Jews upon the authentic traditions of Egypt itself.

Not everything they read in Manetho would have been that palatable, the source of many a later antisemitic conspiracy theory. They could hardly have liked the statement of the descent of the Jews from Lepers. But, this aside, they were also able to identify their ancestors with the Hyksos, and the Exodus with the expulsion of these invaders (Waddell xvi).

The Pillars of Seth

In what Lloyd Graham calls the "pseud-epigraphal" Seth, who was taught the secrets of the Eden world from his father Adam. This he then inscribed on pillars or tablets in order that they survive the predicted flood, which would eventually wipe out the family line of Cain. Josephus records a similar idea in his publication *Contra Apion*, that Seth and his descendants would inscribe the secrets of the heavens on pillars. Josephus, following Manetho, seems to associate these pillars with the famous monuments of Seti First at Abydos. Abydos was one of the oldest holy places in the known world, the location of a famous subterranean oracle shrine, built into the buried pharaonic remains, which do indeed record events from humanity's most ancient past. More of this below.

3. The Sphinx Enigma

Anyone exploring this territory will soon be asked for an opinion on the Pyramids and the Sphinx. I recall a conversation with one respected if controversial author, where this was virtually the first question he asked, how old do you think the Pyramids of Giza are, do you follow the orthodox view of them being a product of the Egyptian Old Kingdom, or do you, he said, his eyes sparkling, think they are much older, from the nameless aeon, 10,000BCE? Still now it is for many in my peer group, a shibboleth of spiritual faith. We are all what are sometimes rather snobbily called "Pyramidiots". My response was probably a disappointment though he took it in good part. I don't think my view should be a source of

Giza Pyramids, left is Khafre, right is the Khufu. The Sphinx could be a symbolic entrace to the underworld, the deepest mysteries those of the double headed lion Aker.

Egyptian Predynastic ceramic dish now in Antiquities Museum, Cairo. Before writing but lends itself to interpretation as the sun's journey from dusk to dawn through the mountains of the underworld. Precursor to later written books of the underworld journey. Nagada I/Amratean period circa 4000 bce

disenchantment, far from it. My view is, in my opinion, more magical, more enchanting but in an informed way. I think I can even link this issue to the topic of the Nephilim, it may even make more sense of it. I have a view that I believe is useful to us in terms of today's philosophy and magick.

You're, dear reader, are no doubt aware of the theory of amateur Egyptologist John Anthony West (1979), in *The Serpent and the Sky* which is based on supposed water damage to part of the sphinx, which is posited as evidence of its extreme antiquity. The flood damage on the limestone sedimentary layers into which the Sphinx is cut, and other flood damage, led him to propose a time much earlier than the orthodox view on the date of the Pyramids. And as the Sphinx enclosure is an integral part of the entire Giza plateau, it has been reasoned that the entire complex could be older, even pre-Egyptian, ie Atlantean in construction. There are various permutations of this view, either shocking, perhaps even preposterous. The following aerial view of the Sphinx shows the main features that West focussed on.

Armed with this theory one can then continue to look for more enigmas and anomalies on this site, and experts who might add to the theory. Pretty soon every aspect of the orthodox chronology of Egypt, and the sequence of the many other pyramids is questioned. But I believe it is a classic *castle in the air*. Guided tours of the Cairo museum make a point of stopping before the diminutive statue of King Khufu, third king of the Old Kingdom's 4th dynasty. At just a few centimeters high, we are asked to believe this is the only relic that connects him to the nearby pyramid, which is Egypt's largest. The paucity of finds from within the pyramids is seen as yet more negative "evidence" that they were never built as funerary moments or tombs but have some other, prehistory reason for their existence. If anything, so the argument goes, the later Egyptian kings appropriated, as they often indeed did, monuments that were already in existence long before the Egyptian civilisation formed.

Conventionally the Sphinx is seen as part of the pyramid complex of Khafre, son of Khufu. The causeway to his pyramid is entangled with the Sphinx. Some experts say it was original part of an earlier temple complex to the sun, which Khafre reused for his own monumental construction. You can perhaps see why this might also interest me, in this exploration of Egyptian myths of a previous lost creation. In a nutshell, did they, the Egyptians that is, have a similar theory about their own existence, that it was vastly old? Did they they incorporate their views into the decorations of all their important monuments, perhaps even here at Giza.

This is the *archaising* tendency we encountered before in connection with the temple of Edfu. This is seen everywhere in Egypt from the very earliest monuments, so we should be on the look out for it at Giza. We might think of it as an homage to the past, an acknowledgement of a once golden age, which many cultures look back to.

There's a clear example of this in Khufu's great pyramid. There are three main chambers in his pyramid. A King's, and a socalled Queen's chamber, though no queen was ever buried there, rather they were routinely accommodated in satellite pyramids clearly visible on plans of the site. There is also a subterranean vault carved into the bedrock beneath the whole structure. Once again we have the motif of a buried archaic space, a symbolic *underworld of the soul*. The subterranean chamber may look unfinished but this is probably intentional, it all adds to the sense of an older space incorporated by the Egyptians themselves into the complex. It is a mind game if you like, and one that one encounters all over Egypt in its monuments.

If you look at the aerial view again you can see the Sphinx, certainly the oldest colossal sculpture known from Egypt and arguably elsewhere. Design wise it is a bit clunky, an early experiment in form, the body too long and the head too small. One of those problems of the sculptural art, how to carve a human head on a lion's body, given that a lion's head is bigger than a human one. To give you some idea of the scale, a human head would fit in the mouth of a lion. The solution to the artistic problem was to make the human head disproportionately large, but this comes in later versions of the human headed sphinx, a popular theme in Egyptian art.

The depression in which the Sphinx sits was once a quarry, in which the builders removed all the layers of usable stone, leaving a central *berg* of rock which could then carved into a sphinx. Unfortunately they hit a geological fault which probably accounts for some of the awkward angles.

I suppose one would expect that they would excavate a regular rectangular depression with the central part ready for finishing into a sphinx. But you can see that the walls of the depression are actually an irregular rhomboid, with the causeway or path intended to connect to the temple at the edge of the Nile flood plain to the pyramid temple just north of pyramid entrance, on the arid plateau at the top. Here began the cultivated area of the site, where there was, once upon a time, an artificial harbour. This causeway passes along one side of the Sphinx enclosure. This is why it is said that the Sphinx is integrated into the whole design, and must have been made with this in mind, ie at the same time as the pyramid, which actually used some of the same stone quarried from around it.

There is an argument that the sphinx and the causeway were already present as part of an earlier ritual complex, known to Khufu and reutilised by his son Khafre for his pyramid (Reader 2005). This would have been an early circa 3000BCE perhaps even predynastic settlement. This would be another example of the incorporation of an ancient, archaic looking construction into a newer one. The walls of the Sphinx depression are eroded with what looks like water damage, you can see the little dried paleo channels running through it, and these same patterns are visible on the Sphinx and elsewhere on the Giza plateau, at for example the Valley temple of Menkaure, which sits on same rocky strata.

This supposed water damage is said by some geological experts, notably Robert Schoch (1992) to be evidence of torrential rain, and it is assumed that this is from a rainy period in the far distant past long before the unification of Egypt. It could also be evidence of a Tsunami etc etc.

"Flood damage at Menkaure's valley temple (Reiser 1931) attest to the fact that even during the late Old Kingdom, rainfall runoff was a significant agent of erosion at Giza" (Reader 2005) During one discussion online I asked the obvious question, "how do you know it wasn't raining when the pyramids were built?" thinking to be shot down immediately, but it was seen as a reasonable question, evidence of ancient climate being precisely what we are looking at, there was no Meteorological office in the ancient world. All we can say is that if what we see is ancient water erosion then this must have happened after they were built. For many this is where doubt creeps in as to when this might have been. Was it really built for Khufu? Skeptics point out that his only surviving link with the site is a tiny statue, just a few centimeters high, now proudly displayed in the Cairo museum.

Another interesting thing came up in my twitter exchange, the well informed person talked about how the Pyramids at Giza when opened were found to be full of salt damage associated with being flooded. It reminded me again of the Nephilim myth we have been exploring and also the fact that Egyptian builders had no damp course, the opposite, they placed the foundations of many buildings on the shale aquifer that runs through Egypt. This was obviously a symbolic thing that overruled any thoughts of wanting a dry building. They wanted to make contact with something underground, which for them was the flood at the beginning of time. They did this and kept doing it all through their history, despite the problems it might have caused. I think I first mentioned this aspect of symbolic building in my pioneering book on this magick viz *Tankhem*. But it's always worth reminding myself, and you good reader, of this intriguing tendency. It is the same story being referred to again and again. And it's the Egyptians telling it, to themselves and to their future selves.

And of course not forgetting the subterranean chamber under the Khufu pyramid, not some abortive design but part of the original conception.

It makes far more sense to me that the Pyramid do this in the orthodox, historical time frame. And rather startlingly, when the Egyptians had no real artifacts from their prehistory to show, they just went ahead and had some made. Unbelievable? To show how this might be the case the best example you have to look at comes from Abydos, which was the necropolis of Egypt's earliest kings, before the opening up of Saqqara and Giza. It even has its own proto pyramid, if the stepped mastaba tombs are those. Before turning to Abydos, I must share another remarkable and recent archaeological find, which in my opinion changes everything, and whilst not well known but deserves to be.

The Red Sea Scrolls

A remarkable discovery of recent years concerns the Red Sea harbour used by Khufu's workforce to source copper for his mason's tools, but also, returning for a semester at the Tura quarries near Giza. Here they were part of the workforce that transported stone by boat to the pyramid harbour, where, all told, an estimated 28 large stone blocks, each weighing approximately 2.5 tonnes were delivered every day.

Amongst the organic remains found at the site are what is now the oldest surviving Egyptian papyrus, the apply named, Red Sea Scroll, which is the rather unpromising mariner's logbook, full of fascinating insights into the mechanics of building Khufu's pyramid. This papyrus fills the vacuum of information about Khufu into which so much speculation has fallen. (Tallet, Lehner 2021)

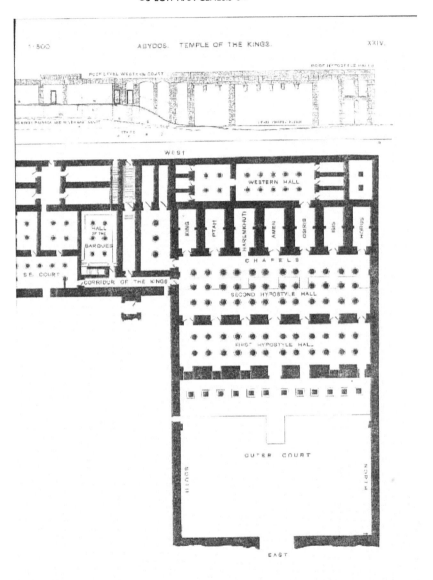

4. Abydos & the Giant

OK so Abydos, which was the royal cemetery of Egyptians first dynasty kings such as King Den. It is one of the world's most remarkable ancient places, and a major pilgrimage site whose beginnings are lost in the mists of time. One of its surviving treasures is the mortuary temple of Seti the first, the second king of the 19th Dynasty. In his time, the capital of Egypt had moved to Waset, modern Luxor in Upper Egypt, whose elites buried their dead in the Valley of the Kings. Sety's luxurious tomb is there, and he was fortunate enough that his body actually remained in this tomb for a while, until it too was moved to a cave, to protect it from the ancient tomb raiders. His magnificent alabaster sarcophagus graces the John Soanes museum in London. Soanes was a freemason, who bought it from the adventurer Belzoni after it was turned down by the British Museum! It seems it was customary for Egyptian kings to have several funerary monuments. In addition to his tomb in the Valley of the Kings, Seti had several mortuary temples. One of these is at the west bank village Gurna, Luxor. But the finest and one of the world's masterpieces, is at Abydos. They are often confused.

The Abydos temple plays a remarkable game

© mandrake of oxford

with the observer, which tells you that someone actually expected an observer of the future to notice all this seemingly buried material. As is well known, the temple has a unique L shaped ground plan, quite different to his other temple at Gurna. The conceit is

The view to the west and the gap in the cliffs called Pega, the entrance to the underworld.

© mandrake of oxford

The ground floor of the Osireion looking to the west, the steps to deeper levels flooded as intended.

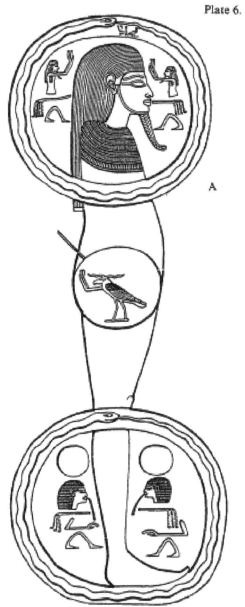

Plate 6.

A

The Osireion had an image, now destroyed by ground water, shows the Giant Osiris, unified with the sun god Ra, his head in the Upper Regions, his feet in "place of destruction". This would have been similar to the above image from Tutankhamun's golden shrine which shows the Egyptian precursor of Abraxas, complete with ouroboros serpent.

that during the building process, as Seti's masons extended westwards they encountered unusual ground conditions. Investigating they found another much older building underground, which, one can surmise they said, was none other than the tomb of Osiris! Indeed such are the number of tombs and temples at Abydos that building new on older foundation is quite feasible. Indeed further out west in the desert, is a first dynasty tomb of Menes or Narmer, the first pharaoh of a unified Egypt, whose tomb is at Umm el Qaab, that was over time treated as if it were also the tomb of Osiris.

The Arabic name Omm el Qaab "mother of pots" is an indication of how extensive was the pilgrimage here … all leaving votive pots of bread and beer. So what of the supposed tomb found by the masons building Seti's temple? This was the subterranean structure known as the Osireion. Some call this a "resurrection chamber" which is therefore very central to Alchemy. More of this in my *Magick of the Sky*. (forthcoming)

The Osireion Giant

An important, enigmatic image of the Giant Osiris Ra was in the important sarcophagus room at the eastern most end of the Osireion or cenotaph. The water that was so much part of this resurrection chamber has made many of the inscriptions illegible.

But from what traces remain, many of them coded text, we know there to have been an image similar to that of the giant seen in several tombs in Valley of the Kings. The most spectacular example was found in the tomb of Tutankhamun, as it appears on the second of his golden shrines. This same giant recurs in a great many New Kingdom tombs, crucially that of Ramses VI.

This structure is connected with a whole stream of occult knowledge called alchemy in the Arab world, known as *Hiera techne* in Greek Egypt. According to the *Book of Enoch,* as quoted by Manetho, it was one of the skills taught to the daughters of men by the Nephilim. The mother and father of psycho-physical alchemy was Zosimus of Panopolis and his partner Theosebeia. Their unique adventures are told in a recently discovered copy of Zosimus's *Book of Pictures* (Mushaf as-suwar). He served as a technician priest at the temple of Min at Akhmin/Panopolis in Egypt. His skills of colour making are intimately connected with the inner secrets of Alchemy, where for example, metals are tinted to appear like gold. Akhmin is very close to Abydos, and it seems likely that the resurrection chamber there and in other Egyptian temples, played a role in the development of a similar entity with Alchemy. (Fuad & Apt 2011)

The chamber is sunken deep into the ground so

that it lies on the natural aquifer, the geological layer of shale that runs through the Nile valley and carries the subterranean flood plain running under the desert either side of the river valley. It is a water filled place of mystery, looking very like an archaic tomb, but on a superhuman scale, with architectural "quotes" in terms of style, some possibly borrowed from the Sphinx temple at Giza, even down to the utilization of the same kind of granite pillars. From its earliest beginnings, the mysteries of water were very central to Egyptian religion, as much as they are still in its alchemical legacy.

The Osirieon looks like an ancient place where Osiris might have been first drowned and later decapitated by Seth. This is the dissolution side of the alchemical equation, the "demonic" transformation or initiation of Osiris, by Seth. But also the kind of place where the process might be reversed. This was a horrific, taboo event to the Egyptian mind but this did not stop them reenacting it as a mystery play in various cycles and epicycles through the year. A related text would be the *Amduat*, "the hidden chamber" or "what is in the underworld".

So the ground level temple was redesigned on an apparently *ad hoc* basis, supposedly, giving it its L shaped footprint known today from the well preserved remains and archaeological plans. The builders even incorporated apparently abandoned, truncated crypts in a different style, as if overtaken by the changed plan.

So what of the Osireion, it is really older than the temple above. Archaeologists confirm that every feature was constructed at the same time as the main temple. It is the equivalent of the subterranean "abandoned" chamber beneath Khufu's pyramid which was perhaps another "resurrection chamber". It is also the case that some early dynastic or predynastic structures were incorporated into its foundations, for example, a prehistoric grain parcher was found here, part of the way ingredients such as water and grain were reprocessed into sacramental beer. So Osiris as "John Barleycorn" the spirit of the corn, lives on.

The sacred deception continues, as this tomb is decorated with some of the most important astronomical texts in all our history. These include the *Book of Nwt*, whose content so confused and revolted its first modern readers soon after its discovery. The sealed transverse chamber, contained two additional scriptures of hers, in addition to the one already mentioned and is thus in effect an entire shrine of Nwt, the *colossal* starry mother of the gods, whose name actually means "watery one".

One of these stone books contains a version of the ancient Egyptian lunar calendar, but of a kind that had already fallen into disuse at the time it was

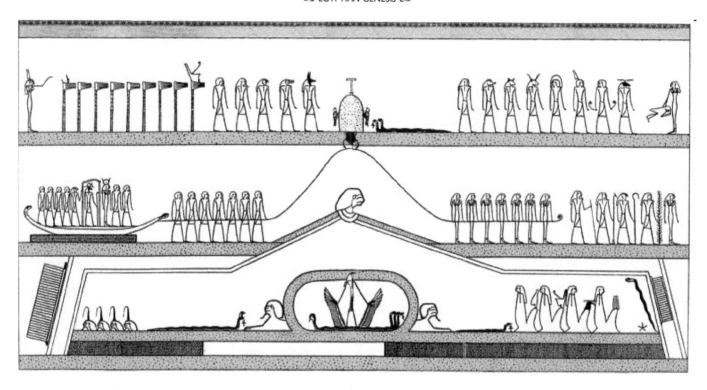

Pyramid mysteries explained in this New Kingdom scene from the Amduat. #393 ... "Flesh of Sokar-upon-his-sand" - Sokar-Osiris in the pyramid shaped burial chamber supported on double headed sphinx (Aker). The Egyptian of New Kingdom- the head at the peak is "The Flesh of Isis" ... indeed the heart of the mysteries in Egypt (information from Kreikamp, *Amduat, the great awakening*)

carved in Seti's temple. It also contains an even earlier version of the same lunar calendar. Like many Egyptian astronomical monuments, they often are like a clock set with the dial running backwards, pointing to a very early time. So I can repeat, this is a thing, the Egyptians built the pyramids and the Sphinx, but they also built the "atlantean" myth of an older, buried civilisation, traces of which were often literally under the floor.

5. The Seriadic Land

Returning to Manetho, whose name recurs over and over in this story. The material of his *Egyptiaca* (History of Egypt), was, according to the version found in Syncellus, obtained from monuments lying in the "Seriadic land", another name for Egypt. The same version also tells us that the Nephilim taught Alchemy, known then as *Hiera Techne*, sacred technology, such as the "Resurrection Chamber". This they taught to woman, ie the "Daughters of Men".

This term could well be related to Sai'di or Sahidic, meaning people who live in Upper Egypt. Sahidic is an important dialect of the ancient Coptic language, also known as Thebaic, all from the same region. So the pillars were inscribed in the sacred characters by the god Thoth. Either way, Manetho in his *Book of Sothis* (Waddel : 209), claimed to have seen these records and then

translated them into Greek. It is all looking entirely possible.

Given all these links, it seems there are many clear examples of the Jews, as they were engaged in translating their Talmud into Greek, including the section concerning the Nephillim, were at the same

Left : An image of Ptah, Above: Image of Imhotep from El Kab, but wearing the same distinctive headdress. Imhotep was chief arhetech on Dsoser pyramid and was an early avatar of Ptah, the great architect

The ancient Serapeum at Saqqara and one of his gigantic Sarcophagi of the Apis Bull cult, later revived as Serapis.

time, engaged in a dialogue over several ancient Egyptians chronologies.

Another summary of Manetho's *Aegyptiaca* chronology comes from Bishop Julius Africanus (Waddell: 27) reads "In succession to the spirits of the dead, the demigods, the first royal house number eight kings, the first of whom [after the flood] was Mene of Thinis, who reigned for 62 years. He was carried off by a hippopotamus and perished."

Manetho also gets several mentions in the PGM (III 440 and PGM XIII 1-343) in for example "A sacred" or "unique" or "Eight Book of Moses". Moses was the focus of a popular magical cult in Roman Egypt. Manetho was often cited as the author of other equally powerful magical books, and is even credited with the creation of the important late Osirian cult of Serapis.

All these Egyptian records make a point of mentioning the physical size of those early King. Thus Manetho, as quoted by Syncellus in turn quoted in Africanus (Waddell: 37) wrote that a king known as Sesostris, usually identified as King Senwosret of Egypt's 12th dynasty (1991–1778 BCE) "ruled for 44 years and his stature was 5 cubit 3 palms. Which is very tall, almost 8 feet! Senwosret was a warrior king, very famous in antiquity for his martial exploits, so there could be some hyperbole in this account. (see also Diodorus Siculus 1, 44, 4.)

Other sacred Egyptian texts, such as that that accompanies the 7th hour of the *Amduat*, echo this idea that "Every living creature has emerged from his, (Atum's) flesh, which is emphasized by his enormous stature." This particular underworld book often comes up in these kinds of considerations. He is the One from whom the many emerge, and would have to be enormous for that to be possible.

So according to Manetho, the "first man (or god) in Egypt was called Roman Vulcan or Greek Hephaestus, by which he is thought to mean the Egyptian god Ptah. Primus Homo (deus) Aegyptiis Vulcanus" (Eusebius), Egyptian Ptah or Etruscan Sethlans.

Incidentally, Hephaestus is mentioned in the account of Atlantis recorded in Plato's dialogues, the longest version being that of *The Critias* (106a sq). Here's a quote:

"Now different gods had their allotments in different places which they set in order. Hephaestus and Athene, who were brother and sister, and sprang from the same father, having a common nature, and being united also in the love of philosophy and art, both obtained as their common portion this land, which was naturally adapted for wisdom and virtue; and there they implanted brave children of the soil, and put into their minds the order of government; their names are preserved, but their actions have disappeared by reason of the destruction of those who received the tradition, and the lapse of ages."

Manetho, whose account we are examining, followed what is nowadays labeled the "Memphite" theology, whose primary deity was Ptah, known to the Greeks as Hephaestus. Egypt had no unified theological schema, there were lots of parallel systems. Judging by the Coffin Texts, every individual could validly construct their own variation, perhaps within certain ground rules. So for him, Ptah was the top god, whereas for others it was Atum, or Ra, or Amun. Many of these pantheons or *enneads*, are otherwise, pretty similar.

The Heliopolitan version of the theology of ancient Memphis, is known from an artifact called the Shabaka stone, which itself tells us that it is a copy, of "a work of the ancestors, preserved on a worm eaten papyrus". Ptah was the local cult deity of ancient Memphis, whose Egyptian name was Inebu-hedj (the White Walls). Not much remains of ancient Memphis but it must have been located somewhere in the vicinity of modern Giza in Greater Cairo.

According to Manetho, Memphis was founded by Egypt's renowned first human King, Menes. The kings in Manetho's earliest list comprise all of the male deities of this well known "theology". One may wonder why the female gods were never female pharaohs? Elsewhere Manetho does records the reign of Egypt's human female pharaohs, including Skemiophris; better known as Sobekneferu, who reigned for 4 years. He knew there were others, so their omission of goddesses from the rule of the gods, is not chauvinism but likely down to this was the tradition as he knew it.

After Ptah came Helios (the sun god or Ra), then Sosis (Shu), Chronos (Geb), Osiris, Typhon (Seth), Horus (son of Osiris and Isis). Another version, known as the Turin King list, also begins with the reign of the gods, so it's safe to say this is how the Egyptians viewed their beginnings. The pantheons may differ a little according to source, the Turin list for instance begins with Horus kings, Ra, Shu, Geb, Osiris, Seth, Horus, Thoth, Maat, and again Horus; but in all examples, kingship begins in the divine realm.

Ptah, is one of the great gods of Egypt, though, judging by archeological records, is not indigenous but may be a loan from elsewhere in the semitic Near East. He wears the distinctive skull cap, seen elsewhere in predynastic icons. His name, meaning "the opener", comes from records from before the Pyramid age. An important manifestation of his cult would be in the Apis bull, whose colossal, indeed gigantic sarcophagi may still be seen at the Serapeum of Saqqara, which is close to ancient Memphis.

The Old Chronicle

It is clear that the Egyptians committed most of their important records related to chronology to stone. So yet another monument, relevant to our study is the so-called Palermo stone, an exported artifact now in the Sicilian museum at Palermo .

Its historian finds that, "Lacking realistic data on lengths of reigns of their early kings, ancient chronologers of the court tradition had perforce to rely upon symbolic astronomical concepts. Thus the king was viewed as the earthly counterpart of heavenly Sirius and his earthly reign needed to be 19 or some factor thereof." (Omara 1979 : 2/23). This 19 year cycle is the interval between the morning heliacal rising of Sirius and any new moon.

Another example of symbolic chronology is found on the walls of the temple of Hathor at Dendera where it says "On the 21st day of Khoiak, the god Osiris attended by images of 34 deities made a mysterious voyage in 34 tiny boats made of papyrus, illuminated by 365 lamps."

One might ask why 34, it seems a bit arbitrary? But now, thanks to analysis of the Palermo stone, we know why: some Egyptians used a 17 (or 34 (2/17) year cycle, from archaic times, which in this case, is the coincidence of the heliacal rising of Sirius with a full moon. In other words, the star Sirius will begin its annual rising at dawn on a full moon but only every 17 years. All these hidden cycles play a role in Manetho's theorising. The double dating by two astronomical coordinates also provides a useful clue as to the construction of certain monuments, such as the great pyramid at Giza, which can be so coordinated to approximated 3600BCE.

Barbarus, quoting Manetho, says that Hephaestus ruled 680 years (which is 17x40). This is how his chronology works, in the absence of empirical observations there are symbolic coordinates that nevertheless do have some relation to natural events.

Syncellus, another writer, who despite quoting him unreliably, was heavily reliant on Manetho and gives the period of time from Adam to the flood as 2242 years. This he says is in accordance with scripture, by which he means the Jewish authorities. One of the apostles, also alludes to these records when in (Luke iii.36) he presents his genealogy of Jesus Christ.

Just to make things more tricky, these ancient contemporaries trashed each other's work. Thus Syncellus said that Africanus had added 20 years to this figure and was thus less reliable than his version. Despite this, O'Mara, a modern scholar, actually finds Africanus the more reliable of ancient chronographers!

So roughly speaking, they all thought that the years from Adam to the times of Abraham was around 3202 years, or 960 years after the flood. This number may work for Jewish history but only as part of a much greater time frame.

Syncellus says the 30 Egyptian dynasties with 113 generations comprise 36,525 years, which is 25 x Sothic cycle of 1461 years. Remembering that the Sothic cycle of 1461 years, the number of years it takes for Sirius to rise at dawn, (heliacal) on the morning of any fixed event, such as one particular New Year New Moon closest to the beginning of the calendar year. "In his study of Egyptian calendars Parker concluded that the cycle of 25 years had been introduced in the fourth century BCE (*Calendars* 1950 : 22-23). 309 lunations = 9125 days = 25 Egyptian years – which was well known in ancient astronomy and used in Ptolemy's *Almagest* VI, 2, where lunar tables are always arranged in groups of 25 years.

Six dynasties = 11,628 or (17x19x36)

"The Palermo Calendar shouts out the claim that the civil calendar was established at the end of the reign of King Djoser" (O'Mara 1979: 2: 39) In other words the construction of the first pyramid, the Djoser "step" version, marks a big change in terms of space and time, and becomes year zero of a new calendar system.

Either way, the rule of the gods (or proto-humans) was said to be 13,900 years. Another significant number in so many ways. These antique accounts tell us that the numbers, though said to be of years for each dynasty of gods, when actually lunar months, each of 30 days, is meant. This would be the time the moon takes to pass through the entire cycle of the Zodiac. But, scholars say there is no evidence that the Egyptians ever thought a year lasted the equivalent of a lunar month. So this is more likely an example of Jewish commentators, who made an epitome of all three his three books, "correcting" Manetho, in order to make the chronology fit more closely with their own Biblical tradition.

If you take all these numbers together from first man to the time of the flood, the total come to 24,900 years. If you convert to lunar months it comes to 2206 years, which is very close to the traditional Hebrew chronology of 2242 from Adam to the flood. In other words, the Jews of the time worked their history on a much shorter time scale, with for example Moses being just over the horizon of living memory. With hindsight, and in the light of modern archaeology and geology, we may find some of these timelines from creation to the Roman era, to be absurdly and unnecessarily brief.

The number 24,900 seems more credible if only because it gives us more time in which to fit all these historical and prehistoric events. But, as this turns out it has its own significance, as I am sure the reader is well aware by now. It is the number of years it takes for the sun to make its precession through all the signs of the Zodiac, due to a "wobble" in the Earth's rotation giving rise to complex variations in the cycle known as precession. The precession cycle is 1 degree every 72 years or some authorities say 25920 years. I'm not going to overcomplicate things by discussing that now. Suffice to say, when Manetho said the rule of the gods was measured in years of 365 days duration, he probably meant it.

After the rule of the gods, comes a shorter period (1255 years) when Egypt was ruled by the demigods. Again, we have other speculations, mostly from Jewish commentators, which we learn of via the Essenes, and their *Book of Enoch*, which abounds in astronomical speculations. They said that as time passed from the beginning, the length of the year had increased. From our perspective it is difficult to understand why they felt the need to make such an argument about the length of the year. Why burden yourself with such a ridiculously small time frame in which to fit human history? But as I said earlier, it all served to give it the sense of being within living memory, whereas in the modern era we like to think we have a better sense of perspective. But there again, how many times have I seen Aleister Crowley written about as if he were still alive, when he is dead more than 70 years!

The Horoi

Anyways, these same Jewish commentators said that during the reign of the "demigods", which they gleaned from Manetho, a year only lasted the equivalent of three lunar months, something called a *Horoi*.

But Pingree, quoting an Indian source, tells us that a Hora or Horoi is an even shorter period of time, meaning half a zodiacal sign; represented by two images per sign (Pingree 1963). The Indian version of the Horas, is very tantrik as one can see from these examples:

"The 1st horas of Aries wears red clothes and is flaming like the sun at doomsday. He holds a sword and a firebrand in his hands. Half of his hair is tawny and his earrings are of gold. He is a fierce man who has raised the staff of death for the sake of protection"

"The first horas in Virgo is a black and white woman who is charming and wise. She is wet with her menstruation and has filthy garments. She thinks of fine clothes, and desiring a son, has intercourse with the man she loves.

She cries in the forest among the serving girls of Brahma, leaning on a branch that is full of fruit and leaf. She is in distress and is without money and her body is stretched out. She has attained beauty."

The whole text, which can be difficult to come by can be found in the Appendix.

Perhaps what is meant is that different demigods ruled different months or half months of the year, rotating on a cycle. This would actually fit with the old Egyptian ritual year where the months were "god bearing" i.e. named after Egyptian gods. It could also be a reference to the personification of the hours of the day and night by different demigods.

Whatever, all of this reducing solar years to lunar months, and their symbolism is another of the things that the *Egregori* or watchers taught humans or at least their daughters. The watcher is another name for the Nephilim in the *Book of Enoch*.

"From the creation of Adam indeed down to Enoch, ie to the general cosmic year 1282, the number of days was known in neither months nor years; but the Egregori (or "Watchers"), who had descended to earth in the general cosmic year 1000, held converse with men, and taught them that the orbits of the two luminaries, being marked by the twelve signs of the Zodiac, are composed of 360 parts". (Syncellus quoted in Manetho 2004: 11)

So after the rule of the gods in Egypt came two consecutive groups of rulers for Egypt, the "demi gods" and the "Spirits of the Dead". The "Demi gods" are most likely a well known group in Egypt called "The Followers of Horus" known in the native tongue as the Shemsu Hor or Falcon Clan. And as these are mentioned in apposition to "the Spirits of the Dead" we can surmise that this second group refers to the Confederates or Companions of the god Seth, the *Smaout en Set* or the "Hippo" clan. This term "spirits of the dead" is still a strange one, and may refer to the heterodox burial practices which were revealed by Petrie in the cemeteries associated with the ancient citadel of the Nubt, or Ombos, near the modern Egyptian town of Nagada. These people did not mummify their dead, and lived cheek by jowl with their ancestors, much as modern Cairo residents live in the legendary "City of the Dead", known as Babylon by the Romans.

These ancient people who buried their ancestors under or close to their houses, will be a topic to return to in conjunction with the supposed fate of Nephilim, who in Biblical and Egyptian sources were buried under the floor.

So "Spirits of Dead" were, as we said, probably followers of "Seth-Typhon", part of the "Hippo" clan. The name seems entirely appropriate for the god Seth, who is a very ambiguous, queer deity, often viewed as the personification of evil. As well as their special death customs and a closeness of ancestral spirits, they practiced magick and what we might call necromancy, or knowing things by communion with the dead. One way or another, if they were the offspring of the Nephilim, they are also Nephilim.

Seth, though often depicted in miniature form, is really a large god, more powerful than the others, and able to wield a colossal and miraculous spear, fabricated as it is, from meteoric iron, from the sky, the same place from which the Nephilim originate.

The ancient chronicler Manetho is really telling us that for a time in prehistoric times, Egypt was "ruled" by the Typhonians or Sethians. This is essentially true. Actually Manetho also seems to hint that this happened twice in the Egyptian timeline, once during the very old times when the actual god Typhon (or Seth) ruled for 45 years. It happened again with the descendents of Seth, the presumed predynastic occupants of the ancient citadel already mentioned. This was a joint rule, a federation with the nearby people of Horus-Falcon and lasted, according to Manetho, for 1255 years.

An uneasy peace existed between the two tribes. Strange as it may seem, there are real ancient memories captured in all this. A renaissance of the rule of the "Spirits of the Dead", may also have occurred during the rule of the Hyksos kings, who were settlers and rulers of Egypt for a 100 year period from approximately 1650BCE. They were also notable as followers of the god Seth.

Whilst on the topic of the Hyksos, there is another connection with the ancient Hebrews. There is a credible theory that the Hyksos, who settled in Egypt but were eventually expelled by resurgent native Egyptian Kings, then fled Egypt eastwards and disappeared from history somewhere in ancient Canaan, where they merged with other local peoples. The Canaanite deity Ba'al shares many features of Seth. This all then feeds into the mythology of the Hebrew deity Jehovah. So much so, that even today, some Israeli researchers claim the Egyptian Hyksos are their ancestors and affirm that the Jewish faith contains some traces of ancient Egyptian Seth.

The demigods or followers of Horus-Falcon are more familiar to us and and were:

Horus

Ares (Montu)

Anubis

Hercules

Apollos

Ammon

Tithoes (Tutu)

Sosus (Shu)

Zeus

When you look at all the extracts and summaries of Manetho that have survived in books of his contemporaries and later writers, the picture is a little confusing, but there are some things that are consistent across all of them. And this is the idea of the prehistoric era, chaotic perhaps, but inhabited by semi-divine, we might say supernatural beings. These were all heroic beings, who lived life on an epic scale.

The House of Life

Every Egyptian temple had what is known as a House of Life (*Per Ankh*), which would have been a centre of religious and intellectual life, a place where the sacred manuscripts were stored, and scribes copied, both as a form of preservation and for the craftsmen tasked with carving these on the walls of temples and tombs. Some of my fellow interpreters of Egyptian mysteries sometimes call it "the hall of records". This would be where initiates into the mystery tradition were inducted and trained.

We already mentioned the Shabaka Stone, its self-description as based on a "worm eaten papyrus". Recopying papyri is the perennial work of all scribes. Consider the scriptorium of the medieval monastery,

brought to life in Umberto Uco's *The Name of the Rose*. Because of the nature of these manuscripts, this was also a place of magick and undoubtedly, the mysteries. This was so, because it was a reserve for the many manuscripts full of formulas and instructions, on all topics. Here were the originals of the sacred books to be copied onto the walls of tombs and temples. Other surviving manuscripts, such as those connected to what is known as "the Harem Conspiracy", document an ancient trial in which the

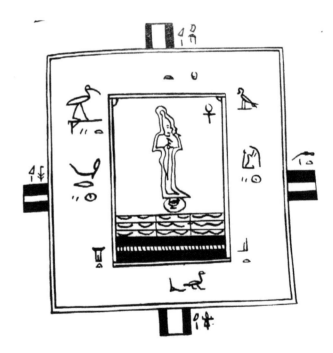

Image of house of life = Osiris in the centre, Thoth in the North (Top Left), Horus South, Isis Nephthys West, Isis East (bottom right), Nwt above, Geb Below

conspirators obtained proscribed works of lethal magick from the temple House of Life. This narrative reads like an ancient version of Shakespeare's *Macbeth*. All this indicates how in many ways the scribe was as important a bearer of Egyptian culture as the priest, perhaps more so.

The building itself was designed as a *theatre* of memory, its shape preserved the order of things, what we might call a geomancy or "mandala" of knowledge. Thus different disciplines were arranged in their appropriate quarter. The *Papyrus Salt* contains a stylised diagram of a House of Life, with Osiris in the centre, four gateways with their different patrons. In my own personal reconstructed House of Life, there are many rooms viz Witchcraft, Companions of Seth; Tantra; Tankhem.

The scribes of the House of Life were privy to, defacto initiates of the wisdom they safeguarded. One can surmise that they must have discussed, as all librarians do, the books they managed, the mysteries if you will. As time progresses, these scribes become the precursors of an international sodality of the wise, like the members of the Hermetic mystery cults, some of which survived the physical destruction of the ancient temples in the early centuries of the first millenia of our era. This memory still lives.

Image of the so-called screaming mummy, who seems to have been kept in the tomb of his victim, Ramses III.

6. The Submerged Ones

It is to the scribes mentioned above and their speculations that we owe many of the stories we have been exploring. This narrative can be reconstructed from the very detailed theological texts they committed to temple walls of the late, so-called Ptolemaic period in Egypt. One of the most comprehensive would be those of the temple of Horus at Edfu, which was an enormous repository of data on ancient material culture, whose techniques included perfumery, colour preparation, the spiritual technology that came to be known as alchemy. Also history, liturgy, architecture and much more besides.

One of these books, or *diaries* in stone is of particular interest to the topic of this book. In a nutshell, it recalls a distant time, what we might recognise as a nameless aeon, long before the development of the hieroglyphic writing system, before even the genesis of the familiar gods of Egypt, before Ra, and Osiris and their children. In this nameless aeon, other unnamed gods ruled.

This is a time even before the famous Falcon god of Egypt. Horus, in whose temple this record is preserved. The name Horus does not directly mean falcon, but something more like "One with a face" or perhaps "Head".

The more usual word used for falcon was "Byk"

We can only theorize that Horus, son of Isis and Osiris, evolved from this god Byk, nothing is certain. All the gods of Egypt seem to have older, prehistoric names. But even before this happened there were other, unnamed gods.

And more, the same text that tells us these things

speak also of a lost kingdom, a submerged place, which was also "the Island of the Trampling", and then "The Island of Peace". These suggestive names or toponyms, point to there being first a trampling, followed by an uneasy peace. This seems to be pointing us towards an ancient, that is to say prehistoric conflict.

The Shebtiw & the Battle at the Beginning of Time

"Your life will be millions of years long and this land will return to the state of the Nun, to the floods which were there at the beginning. I shall destroy everything I have created."
Book of the Dead, Spell 175

Once upon a time, all this information could be read in the many books of the temple library, with titles such the "Sacred Book of the Temples", now

View of the remains of the shrine of goddess Satet on the island of Elephantine. Plan of the original megalithic sanctuary.

The Temple of Horus at Edfu, First pylon looking north-east

lost. What remains are literally the writing on the wall, extracts chosen by the priests for inscription on the Edfu temple walls. In other words the building memorializes its own history via so-called "building texts". Presumably every temple had something similar, but one of the most important and complete versions are those from Edfu.

This famous temple at Edfu was built very late in Egyptian history during the times of the Greek kings, the Ptolemies. Egypt has such a lot of history, it can be difficult to get one's head around all the many milestones in its long timeline. So for example, Cleopatra, enjoyed a relationship with Roman Mark Antony, which also made her the last of the Ptolemies. In 30BCE, a dynasty founded by Alexander Great in 332BCE ended with her suicide.

So the temple would be one of the last ever built in Egypt on a site which archaeologists say was always important, at least for a couple of thousand of years previous, though even then, it is not one of Egypt's primary archaic settlements. That's the current state of knowledge and given the place is being re

The Temple of Horus at Edfu, First courtyard or peristyle hall, symbolic east of the first pylon

excavated, it could all change. But for now we can say that very little happened on this site before the Old Kingdom, in which the first dynasties of Egypt ruled, including those who constructed the pyramids.

Let us assume there was an earlier temple which is now completely built over. It is entirely possibly, that some of the furniture, such as the temple Naos, a highly significant object, was retained from the earlier institution but not much else. The best guess as to how it would look would be from a massive abandoned settlement just 15 kilometers away at a

The Naos of Edfu temple, imitating in stone, a tented shrine. In foreground the barque shrine, on which the diminuitive but precious images of Horus and Hathor could be carried up to the roof on festival days, such as New Year/Solstice sunrise to be revivified, or made "golden" by the rays of the rising sun, "the eastern Ba". (See Lorton)

place known to the Greeks as Hierakonpolis, or the citadel of the hawk.

Strange as it may seem, the oldest shrines would have been stylised tents, huge but essentially portable. Tent shrines should also bring to mind the Israelite tent shrine that they carried with them out of Egypt. The Biblical account is a fairly credible memory of the earliest form of Egyptian sacred enclosure, before things got more formal and built in stone.

Hierakonpolis, was a much older ritual centre which also housed an important shrine to a Falcon god. It is tempting to assume this was the prototype for the Edfu god. We can only guess, as the Horus worshipped there is not exactly the same as at Edfu. If it was the origin, one wonders why such a site, so central to Egyptian history, was ever abandoned?

The Edfu temple is a series of nested tent shrines imitated in stone, one room inside another. Some older architectural forms are conspicuous by their absence. So for example, it does not "quote" or resemble any of the mudbrick shrines of the Old Kingdom. Why the older brick design was discontinued is another mystery. Why would one notable tradition of architecture that had existed for several centuries just stop and disappear? It is as if it has been airbrushed from the architectural repertoire.

So the Edfu builders have chosen a certain style from a number of options open to them. The

Left: the famous statue of Horus outside his temple at Edfu. Right the cult statue of a falcon. Egypt, Hierakonpolis. Dynasty 6, c. 2323-2150 BC. The posture isdifferent and this may be significant. Hammered copper and gold sheet, obsidian, H. c. 55-65cm. Egyptian Museum, Cairo, various JE & CG numbers. (Eckmann and Shafik 2005, fig. 43).

King Khasekhemwy, his awesome mortuary temple at Shunet el-Zebib, Abydos (wikimapia) circa 2780 BCE

foundation of the whole is an island of sand. Buried in the sand is probably the remains of a much earlier shrine. And as we shall see, other even more mysterious things lie buried beneath. Any prehistoric remains would have been discretely incorporated into the existing design, but in such a way that, if you look hard enough, traces can still be seen. This is one of the mind games the Egyptians loved to play.

One notable example was discovered buried in its foundations, beneath the shrine of Satet on Elephantine.

There is a lot of intended meaning here, one that never stops giving in terms of parallel examples each with their own unique message to be revealed in one's meditation. It fills me with immense excitement to learn that the original temples comprised a concentration of natural megaliths, undecorated boulders, obviously special whose significance we have to deduce from empathy and intuition.

The building texts at Edfu allude to this ancient past, the reign of the earth god Tanen who occurs in the Turin King list. This is the time of the rule of the

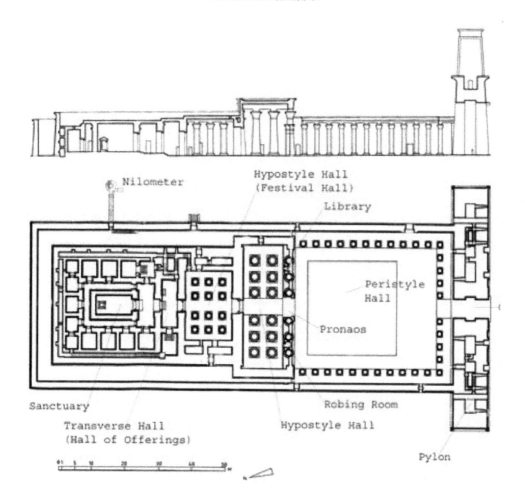

gods, which continued until they were attacked and a separation was required for the safety of both parties. This is part of the background to the material already discussed. Frustratingly, the plans preserved at Edfu are very stylised and geometric. No primitive temples known preserve this precise form but there are points of contact with the archaic cemetery at Saqqara. Every temple in Egypt probably makes a claim to be the original place of creation. They do not appear to be based on any actual archaic shrines, and are likely, according to Barry Kemp, to be a priestly mystical construction (Kemp 1989 : 101).

Which is not an uninteresting thing in itself, we can assume that a certain strata of the priests had time for such meditations and speculations concerning a cosmological nature. They built fantasy temples in their heads which we later committed to papyrus and sometimes were so important, these speculations were carved in stone. Constructing idealized temples may have been the way they visualized the complex cosmology. On a smaller scale perhaps like the old but current practice of designing one's own funeral, is as a statement of one personal piety. A still valuable practice to emulate

Somewhere in the temple at Edfu was a sacred book (*snn* – charter) that contained a complete list of the original sacred shrines collected together with short but appropriate mythological texts. This original book is lost and is only known via preserved extracts, this is pruning by serendipitous loss.

Another of the lost books was called "Specifications of the mounds (*i3t*) of the early primeval age", as with many sacred books, the records claim it was the god Thoth was copied it, after listening to the words of "the Sages of Mehweret" (The Sages of the Great Celestial Waterway). A similar group of Sages is known from the Vedic tradition of India, they who made the *music of the spheres*, remembered by the human authors of the Vedic texts. All of this sounds like very old myth, and therefore strangely connected. The Egyptian scribe also cites the "Sacred Book of the Early Primeval Ones".

So, in our story the first sacred place was marked out on the island of sand. Incidentally, many temples were built on a foundation of sand, even if this made for an unstable construction. *Sand* was often considered as a magical substance, hence geomancy, a form of divination that makes use of such random marks and interprets them. I talked earlier about the temple of Seti at Abydos and its related "Osireion" whose real name, so the experts say, was Menma're "What is serviceable to Osiris". When robbers attempted to break through from there into the hidden room of the upper temple, the sand layer cascaded into their tunnel, a never ending river from the upper foundations, forcing them to stop and retreat.

Thus the temple is a living being, able to respond to those who enter. In the first times, it was the abode of the sanctified ruler, the so called *Heka Netri* (*ḥK3 Ntry*) or great magician. From Edfu we learn that the generic name for the temple is the highly suggestive name, the "Underworld of the soul". The story is all about the moment of separation between the different realms, the world and its underworld, when the later comes into being.

"From all this evidence an important fact emerges: before the actual land of the later historical domains came into existence the Egyptians believed that there existed centres for worship of the ancestors." (Reymond: 168). Edfu was one of those places for the "worship of the ancestor gods at Edfu" (Reymond 1963) . The highly important ritual of the *Opening of the Mouth*, used to animate images of gods and goddesses in the temple also reprises the worship of the ancestor gods.

The scholar Eugene Cruz-Uribe has found the same ideology elsewhere, for example the temple of Hibis (See *Gold of Praise* etc).

One might ponder the psychological meaning of the emergence of the first lands or "mounds" from out of some primal ocean. Such an ocean was a metaphor but also real, in that Egypt's geology is there for all to see, telling us that once upon a time, what is now desert lay beneath an ocean.

This is cosmogenesis, the stories all humans have of the beginning, the genesis of the cosmos, in all its many dimensions. One message is always the same, which would be, it has all happened before, at least once, maybe more than once. In other words, all these stories and a great deal of material from Egypt, advance the idea that there was a *previous creation*. And that for reasons clear and unclear, it was destroyed. Some other modern authors in this genre know these accounts and want to take them literally, as accounts of a real ancient apocalypse.

Perhaps this was so, although there are no remnants that do not fit into the more well known timeline. Inducing the existence of an extremely ancient and advanced "civilization" is, thus far, the work of the imagination. Accounts of it do exist from the Egyptians themselves, just not the artifacts, unless one takes some of Egypt's existing wonders and calls them *heirlooms* from an older time. But this would generate its own problems. It can lead to the absurdity that, as at least one famous author has opined, none of the visual culture of Egypt is actually Egyptian! Ask yourself why no ceramic from this really ancient civilization, not one fragment exists of this significant technology. We cannot answer this question by claiming many Egyptian stone vessels are actually "heirlooms" from the ancient apocalypse, this might well be wishful thinking. And what little that does remain is not more advanced than the Egyptian civilization but is clearly the work of their talented but still less advanced ancestors.

Martialling monuments such as the Sphinx and Pyramids as evidence, claiming they are pre-Egyptian constructions is, in the long run, a delusion, perhaps even an offensive one, and in the end, misses the point.

Here is my solution to the conundrum, which is every bit magical thinking too. In the Egyptian view, as so often in all these stories, there were remnants of those deceased or separated gods somewhere. And because they could no longer be found, the Egyptians, in effect, made replicas. These "remnants" are

Remains of giant archaic statue of Min of Coptos, now in Ashmolean museum Oxford. Ritually decommission-ed in antiquity, thus discovering under the temple floor . The wooden phallus now gone, its placement and removal must have been part of the magical rites. The cup marks are where pilgrims ground powder from the statues for use in healing potions or to absorb magical power. The later a well known magical practice.

incorporated into the foundations of the new temple structures in what for them was a "new world". This is one of the secrets, or metaphors, to which magick of all ages has been pointing and trying to articulate. We live in the second, contingent world.

I already mentioned this in connection with the Sphinx and the Temple of Seti first. I could also add one of the oldest examples of religious sculpture, that of Min, which was discovered buried beneath the floor in the ruined temple of Isis and Min at Coptos, where it had been installed when the temple was still a functioning religious institution. Was this merely recycling and ethical disposal of worn out works, past their best? The Cairo Synagogue's *Genizah* is a similar repository of moribund documents that because of their ritual significance, are buried in a special place. Afterall how does one dispose of the leftover ingredients from a ritual, the answer is carefully.

We could go even further back to the people before they became the Egyptians, living beside what is now a dried out lake in the middle of the Sahara. This is the Napta playa, well worth checking out. This large ritual complex is just the most recent layer, underneath lie sediments and sand from earlier iterations. The archaeologist dug deep beneath the strata, taking us back even further in time, looking for the bedrock. They found a neolithic sculpture,

The Cow Stone, of Napta Playa, Egyptian Sahara. A neolithic sculpture, now in Aswan museum. It was suspended in the sediment, two meters beneath the surface and two meters above the sculpted bedrock. See Wendorf, Fred., Romuald. Schild, and Kit. Nelson. Holocene Settlement of the Egyptian Sahara. New York ; London: Kluwer Academic/Plenum, 2001. Print.

the so-called cow stone, now in Aswan museum. It was suspended in the sediment, two meters beneath the surface and two meters above the sculpted bedrock. Did the people, who would go on to become the Egyptians, even know it was there? Was it the prehistoric equivalent of another notable practice of the old temple builders, the foundation deposit ?

Perhaps there is nothing new in this practice of what we might call archaeological memorialising, where the ancestors are buried under the floor. I'd say it is something we should do more of, at least metaphorically.

It is precisely this trend that is alluded to in the myth of the Shebtiw and the lost, submerged kingdom known as the "Island of the Trampling" and later, presumably after the conflict it is known as "The Island of Peace". This tradition of creation as being involved with some fight, is found in many cultures of the region but not all. Sometimes this tendency is given the rather grand name *Chaos Kampf*, Chaos Struggle, it is a matter of debate as to whether Egypt is one of those cultures. It has to be said that the accounts we are looking at are often fragmentary and entangled with other myths. Kemboly, whose doctoral thesis re-examined some of the material, found it difficult to disentangle all the elements and thought it might just as easily fit with other, more well known creation stories from Egypt.

I am inclined to see it differently. In a nutshell it feeds into a very important issue of the origin of evil, personified for the Egyptians as Apophis. What role does he or she play in creation, if any? For discussion of gender of this ancient entity see my book *Seth and the Two Ways*. It could be, as Kemboly thought, that Apophis was not actually there at the very beginning, and was not part of the original chaos. This is because, in mythological language, Apophis may have a beginning, she was born at a particular moment *after* creation. If so then he or she would, in philosophical language, be a contingent entity. The argument for this comes from only one but important Egyptian account. At Esna Apophis is given a birthday, and is the creation of the goddess Neith, coming forth after the sun god Ra. As we have already noted, one could only take this as the canonical view if it was very commonly expressed. But as it is only one, admittedly important, but late source, it is just a point of view among several, another speculation if you like. Other rival views existed in parallel, including the idea that Apophis was part of the battle at the beginning of time, and is therefore far from contingent, they were there before time began.

This is the meaning of talking about the world before the flood. The "island" world with its temple and a completely alien set of gods, known collectively as the Shebtiw, the "submerged" or lower ones. Which, to me, is pretty much the same class of being as the Nephilim, the "fallen ones", the submerged, or lower. They could also encompass the idea of the world having fallen on them.

It's not such a stretch to see the world of the Shebtiw of Egypt as the parallel to that of the Bible's Nephilim, a world populated by ancient giants, as remembered in later Biblical and Gnostic accounts. It is important to remember that the whole Earth, as it was known then, was likened to an enormous island world, which, even now we sometimes refer to our homeworld in the words of the 1955 Syfy classic as "This Island Earth", floating in space.

We are told that on this island there was a temple, with its own set of gods, known collectively as the Shebtiw – the submerged or lower ones. It can be difficult to determine whether the submerged ones are the victims or villains in an ancient struggle. Over time, we tend to see them, because of their *typhonic* power, as the resident evil. But, given that we are dealing with accounts of very deep and ancient history, it is often the case that the character of vanquished, and those who vanquish them, become confused and transposed in the historical memory.

According to the Egyptian story, there was a time when "darkness was over the island", and darkness also over the primeval waters that surrounded it and eventually submerged it. So the Island-Earth was under the water. There is no dry land anywhere, the world was entirely blue. The Egyptian had a very evocative term of this time, calling it "The Underworld of the Soul". The underworld was always seen as a watery place.

This ambivalent phrase means that events are to be envisioned as actual physical events but they are also somehow things embedded in our psyche for all time. They are the origin of the unconscious mind. They are also the origin of the *underworld* that Egyptians were continually exploring, and for this they did not wait until after death. They made use of several "tourist" guidebooks such as the *Amduat* and the *Book of Gates*, which incidentally tell us that these same books were usable by the living *and* the dead. Wisdom in old Egypt was in part due to a living person's knowledge of these books, from which came knowledge of their own inner being, their selfness perhaps even their future self.

Even if the final journey was unavoidable, there were good reasons to prepare for it and well in advance of actual bodily death. For this, some kind of "death posture" or mimicking death would be necessary. Every Egyptian knew they must make the journey sooner or later. But then, as now, most preferred to avoid the encounter with the *underworld of the soul*, putting it off until the end. Of course after death, the journey can no longer be avoided. It is perhaps characteristic of the magician or adept that they are those who choose not to put off the moment but to actively embrace it, even train for it. This is the utility of studying such works as the *Amduat* and taking time to explore the Osireion in one's imagination. Most of the real action occures in the imaginal realm, whether of dreams, visions or meditation. The physical temples and tombs with their elaborate decoration, essential aids to this process. Learning all this is more than just an interesting intellectual adventure. Recovering and remembering these fragments is the way the mind travels. This is the essence of image magick.

More on the Shebtiw

What do we know about the Shebtiw and how they are arranged? We learned how the remains of perished gods were found near where they fell. And we learn how the Shebtiw came and uttered sacred words that caused the sacred mound to rise again. There are fragments of these ancient spells (*dj3jsw*). These were strange words even to the Egyptians, the *Khenem-aten* and *Tep-towi*. As with so much magick, each person has to recover them anew. Back then they were uttered in special places such as the "Place-in-which-the-Enemies-were-Annihilated" also known as the "Territory of the Ancestor" and "Land of Him who is Great of Arm".

As always, and right on cue, back then, the enemy snake (R^c), who name seems similar to the sun god Ra's, but they are different entities. R^c always appears to try to put a stop to things. Back then it was the magick of the Shebtiw that proved the stronger, too strong for it. Even so there is a tremendous fight before it is driven off.

The Shebtiw had also constructed a shelter, 5 x 15 cubits, though these numbers may be more symbolic than actual. An archaic earth god, referred to a Ptah-tanen, is also protected by two magical staves. The remains of the previous destroyed creation, are heaped up all around or rather beneath, and they glow and radiate as much of their remaining strength allows, thus aiding the new construction.

Eventually a place known as the *pay-lands* are laid out, ten in all, which is a significant number in Egypt cosmology, being a third of a lunar month, the ten days of the week. *Pay* means primeval. Perhaps the original settlements of Egypt, defined by the vast lakes that formed during the inundation. Each *nome* or administrative district of Egypt is dependent on one of these temporary lakes. In Egypt's prime there were many more than ten, but perhaps when settlement started in the Nile valley, there were only ten? Others speculated that this ancient geography refers to something more cosmic or on a larger scale, such as the continents of the earth.

The ten are:

1. The mound of the radiant one
2. The island of Re'
3. The dd pillar of the earth
4. The high hill
5. The oil tree
6. He who is rich in kas
7. Mesen
8. He who makes prosperous places
9. Behdet
10. Place of the ghosts

Next, come a parade of the victorious gods, including the Shebtiw, the original makers of the earth plus The Seven Sages, who may just be another name for the same entities, together with Thoth. Also there are the Seven Builders, with the goddess Sheshat, with her crown of seven rays, who is always there whenever a new template has to be laid out on the ground.

The original primitive enclosure they built was open to the sky with a covered sanctuary at one end. The temple was the material embodiment of its god. The primeval sacred domain existed on ground in which symbols of the creating powers were hidden.

It is again reminiscent of the original tent shrines which were "quoted" in the stone architecture of later temples. Yet another name for this is the "Mansion of Isden", meaning the resting place of the earth

Sacred lake of Mut at Karnak, Google Earth

maker along with four other deities who played a role in the making. His symbols were his mace known as "The Great White", and the Djed pillar, and the image of the front of god. The enclosure was on the edge of the pool, which somehow preserved the concrete shape of the creating powers. All temples in Egypt, no matter how diminutive, have a sacred lake in their enclosure. The pool in the nowadays sealed off campus of Mut at Karnak, has a very distinctive shape, I'd say like a fetus. Anatomical, especially reproductive images abound in Egyptian temple and tomb designs.

Records at Edfu tell us that the first creative power was this Earth god, who could also represented in serpent form, as a snake. Remnants of an ancient serpent cult are dotted all over Egyptian records. This "Primeval one" was already in existence when the world was still in darkness.

Even deeper into the myth, we learn there was a special place at the heart of the Nun, which was the Egyptian name for the chaotic waters from which ultimately everything comes. This is a very abstract, visionary speculation, from magician priests, which says this place was called the "Benent", and it formed within the Nun, as a special substance, just like an embryo. It was created from the mystic union between the Primaeval Ones and the Nun. Once fertilized, the Nun is capable of producing other such substances. Thus the male Primeval ones and female Nun produced an embryonic world. The new born or *fetal* Earth was envisioned as an island (Hieroglyphic *Iw*). Thus we see how similar all these ideas are to the later speculations of the intercourse between the Nephilim and the Daughters of Men.

The Primeval ones (*p3wtyw*) were self-creating, that is to say, born of no womb. At first they were said to be insubstantial, invisible essences, but once the island emerges they can undergo a metamorphosis, taking on physical form, what the Egyptians called a *Djet*.

Some anthropologists see this as the most primitive, in the sense of oldest, cosmology. In this view, the primary matter is the union of water and earth. This differs from doctrines at other centers such as Heliopolis, the equivalent of the ancient *Vatican* in Egypt. Here, perhaps for the first time in the Egyptian timeline, the creative powers, the (*shmw*), were given names that have become familiar to us. For example the sun god Ra, who was born in the pool on the primeval island. And the first island, becomes the embodiment of the lotus, literally a radiance. It is fascinating to learn of the abstract theology that existed before too much codification had occurred.

Decay and resurrection of the island

"The general tone of the Edfu records is of an ancient world, which after having been first constituted, was then destroyed and as a dead world it came to be the basis of a new period of creation, which at first was a recreation and resurrection of what once had existed in the past" (Reymond : 107)

Of the two original domains on the island, that of *Pen* gods and their Djed pillars, and a nameless Creator god, both were destroyed. The mention of Djed pillars brings to mind those supposedly ancestral stones from Gobekli Tepe. Just like those, the Djed pillars bear the ghostlike images of the original ancestors.

So the world was in darkness when the Shebtiw, the descendents of the first makers returned. They found evidence of the fight, which they describe using the familiar metaphor of the sound eye (wadjet) and his fall. Perhaps Eye is referring to the sun or moon. When it fell, all light was extinguished. And the "island" became the tomb of the original inhabitants (*hebebet* water became *w'ret* water). All the surviving names for this place emphasize what happened here, thus the "island of combat" or "of the trampling" etc.

This great battle at the dawn of history, was prefaced by a colossal storm which destroyed the original *Mansion of Isden*. Its very likely that this storm was itself generated by the adversaries in order to weaken the ancestors before the chief enemy made his final assault. This giant attacking serpent was also known as *nehep-wer* "the great leaping one".

Another dedication spell names the enemy snake as Apophis, the well known colossal serpent, who is so like Tiamat or Leviathan. Though this name Apophis is a later euphemism, "the great leaping one" seems likely to be the original.

"Oh thou place in which Apophis was pierced. As the Ka-of-the-earth lives for me, I have constructed for you as my House-of-appearance-in-the mansion-of the god. I have hidden myself in you and I have made you as my great seat in the first sanctuary." Edfu.vi. 319.4-5

These ancient records tell us that the first generation of gods were limited in timespan, they could die, as other gods could also, most famously Osiris. When they were buried in the tombs, it was for other gods or the falcon-like "sages", when they returned to perform rites for them. Which is the origin of all funeral rites.

7. Egyptian Star Maps

One interesting perspective on this derives from the work of Victorian Theosophist Gerald Massey, whose interpretations of the first translations of the *Egyptian Book of the Dead*, (Renouf 1904) are still valued by some contemporary magicians and neopagans. In a nutshell, if you look at the well known star maps of Egyptian tombs, those of Seti I and Semnut being the most famous, a view of the northern sky is presented together with the 36 decans. The group of constellations in the centre were said by Massey to show in effect war in heaven, the principles seven ancient supernatural entities, wrestle for control of the mooring post of heaven, which can be no other than the celestial pole. It is true that over the millennial, the position of the pole star shifts because of a well known phenomena of precession, the wobble in the earth's axis that causes the celestial pole to oscillate on a roughly 25000 year cycle. Some sources, so Massey claimed, say this breaks down into seven segments.

Do Egyptian star maps show this arrangement? On the face of it there are just too many constellations but, if one confines oneself to the central circle, it might just work.

It is a suggestion, the actual text indicates something different, that the entire array of gods, the central ones plus those of the 36 decans, "the spirits of the east", are what is being shown here, the battalions of the sun god through their various stations. The decans, are indeed his army of demonic warriors, in the diurnal struggle, from Solstice to Equinox.

It is those variations in the order of the decans, which one comes first, marking the opening, that does indeed show the Egyptian knowledge of the precession of stars, revolving on a long cycle. In one version, the heliacal rising of Hathor-Sirius occurs near the summer solstice, although in a second version its position has changed and another star of the 36 decans is at the head. This seems clear proof that the Egyptian did know about precession at a very early date.

The cosmic battle shown here in the star-map is more likely that of the annual one between the sun and his enemies. The flood already mentioned, is that

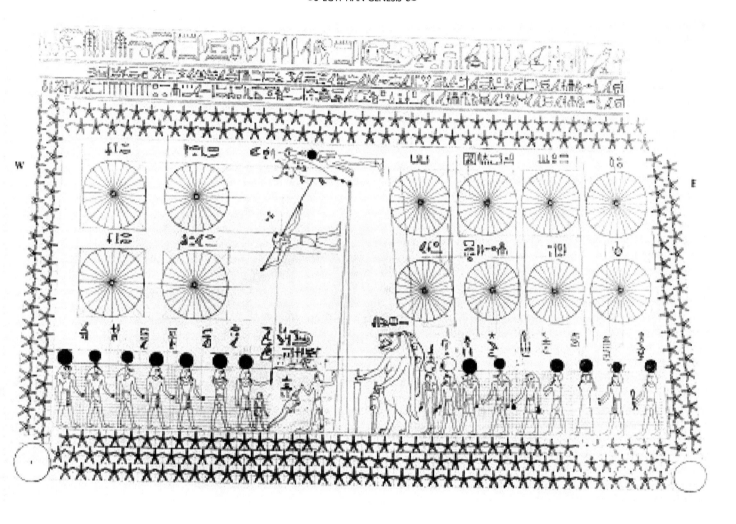

One of the earliest complete star-maps from tomb of Senenmut, a masterpiece of ancient science, created by the gifted Vizier, and technical advisor to Queen Hatshepsut, of the 18th dynasty

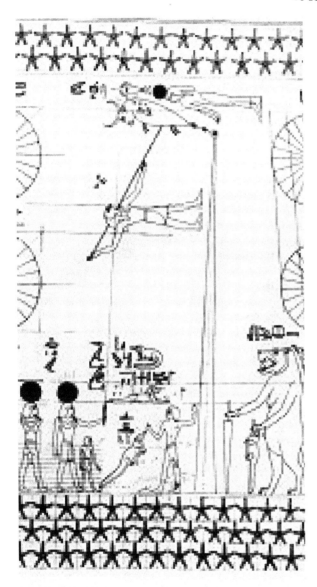

Detail of Senenmut starmap, the pole extended upwards to make space for the Horus spearing Bull-headed constellation Ursa major. Hippo, the constellation Draco, holds the pole.

of the annual Nile inundation. But as with all these records, there may be other aspects to it, and the annual flood is itself a reprise or mesocosm of a more ancient cosmic battle, of the kind recorded elsewhere, including the later myth of the Nephilim and the Shebtiw. The ancient apocalypse would then be foretold in the stars.

The star-maps may indeed record both incidents: the annual cycle and the cosmic flood at the beginning or time, or indeed the seven floods that Massey says occurred at the boundaries between each of the changes of "mooring post" or celestial pole. Why a change of pole would be a catastrophic event is unknown, perhaps when one knows the star markers are changing, there is a *millennial* sense, a human reaction, like the "madness" that overtakes civilization whenever there is a quite arbitrary change, such as a change of millennial or a birthday?

Thus in the version of events from Edfu, which we have been examining, the mythic accounts, are, also, all about the moment the underworld or a new underworld was created. It is as if it was a specific moment in the timeline, when it happened or certainly when we first became aware of the existence of such a thing. Reminding ourselves that things seen in the heavens do have a physical effect on our brains. From a modern point of view, we might explain this as some sort of "engram" or cell of memory locked into the structure of our brains, in the DNA, waiting to be activated. In a sense it is like a false memory that is also a true one. If you prefer a more positivist interpretation, it could be, as I suggested elsewhere, as have others, a neurological thing, something to do with the brain's developments, the connection of one hemisphere with another, or a critical threshold of some kind.

As such it might be something that resonates again, comes to life, whenever we think about certain things or scenarios. It reminds me of those legendary books that one is advised not to read because they are just too evocative. Some stories may be like that. As I understand it, and without buying into all the other things made of it, this is one of the more important and original of occult ideas that lies buried at the core of Scientology. Which would be no surprise given the influence of western magick on its founder, Ron Hubbard. One is coached to visualize certain things from the ancestral memory, some of the scripts are way out there, literal science fiction from the beginning of time. The celebrated monitoring with the E-meter, indicates how one is reacting to them, maybe the heart is racing, and in this instance, one repeats the "memory" until one no longer reacts. Perhaps this is what is meant by becoming *clear*, deconditioned or desensitized.

It is all quite a mental labyrinth, so hardly surprising that some of the original Egyptian accounts were a little unclear about the exact order of these events. The records imply that there have been several catastrophic, existence extinguishing floods. There was a creation but then this has been destroyed and submerged. It could also be a cyclical thing, something that is made and then destroyed several times, each new aeon establishing the magick that makes it endure until time comes around when it must give way or perish. The important number from this point of view is 25000 divided by seven, giving us the number 3500 as the length of each aeon.

Out of the flood, and its lost world emerge the Submerged Ones (the Shebtiw). Or were they present in the beginning, and are submerged but also somehow are those who manage to survive, and, initially weakened, make a comeback when the ancient enemy has momentarily withdrawn? This may have been conceptualized by the Ancient Egyptians as the mooring post is being reestablished.

It would be a very literal view of the mooring post, we are not actually moored to anything, the universe is rotating, but does this have to be in relation to anything, it just rotates?

In terms of modern astronomy the pole marker moves between various constellations and their stars on a long cycle of 25770 years. This slow change is due to the well known phenomenon known as precession of the equinoxes. For some periods the celestial pole points only to empty space, with no obvious star on our sightline. In 3000BCE the polestar was Thuban in the constellation Draco. At around 1700BCE it had moved to Kochab in the constellation Ursa minor. In 300CE, still in the constellation Ursa minor it was the star Pherkad. Currently it is Polaris in Ursa Minor. By the year 3000ce it will be the star Errai in an entirely different constellation Cepheus. It will track through Cepheus for several thousand years. By 8000ce it will be in one of the stars of Cygnus. Then in 14500ce thereabouts it will be one of the stars of the Lyra constellation. Even further ahead in 18400CE it starts to track its way through the constellation Hercules, after which it returns to Draco. In modern terms the path of the polestar touches six constellations rather than seven. However, looking at the older starmaps of Egypt, the constellations are definitely grouped differently, so for example Hippo (see figure) would include Bootes (the Shepherd). In these maps, the image of seven constellations lying on the path of the polestar definitely makes sense.

It is interesting to consider the religious character of predynastic Egypt ruled by Cygnus; 3000BCE Old Kingdom Egypt when the Draco was the celestial pole, and then those of the New Kingdom of circa 1700 bce.

So currently at least the "mooring post" is a star called *Polaris*, but the center could be empty space with no current star marker. This would be inconvenient for navigators, but would not change the dynamics of the universe which would continue to spin regardless. Though poets tend to aver, the lack of a centre is like a universe without a soul.

Two of the Submerged Ones we mentioned are named. They are the ones who will raise the island by the use of magick spells, which back then was a new thing, as this is the moment magick came into the world. The lack of magick, or failure to use it, being the reason the island-earth was overwhelmed in the first place. Magick is the force that makes the continuance of life possible, we live by magick. According to other sources, there were four generations of these unorganized gods and goddesses, that ruled but then fell before the final successful raising of the island, and the beginning of finite time. (Bomhard 2008)

Their names seem strange to us, almost protomorphic. They are basic phonemes such as Aah (the great one) & Wa (the far distant one), like a baby crying. Later in the Jewish *Zohar*, similar names are given to the Nephilim, Aza and Aza-el (see Reymond "Primeval Djeba"). Jeff Lipman of the appropriately named "Garden of Doom" podcast remarked how these are similar to names of the first Pharaoh of

Egypt, Aha, and later Qaa. It has to be said this is all derived from proto-hieroglyphs, signs and symbols on the earliest Egyptian artifacts crafted before the formal language really got going. Their sound can only be reconstructed by a backwards reading of later but similar signs. So their protean aspect may be down to lack of knowledge though it is tempting to think that the first signs in a language have a certain privileged position and reflect the first emotive eruptions of sounds, like seed mantras at the beginning of time. Perhaps all these names are a homage to the Submerged Ones. Back to psychology again, the first expressions, like the computer HAL in the film 2001, who as his memories are deleted reverts to the first song his programmer taught him, the once great machine singing "Daisy, daisy, give me your answer do".

The Shebtiw had this essential role in the resurrection of a whole pantheon of gods rather than one. These mysteries are quoted extensively in the Osireion at Abydos, the best of all the surviving resurrection chambers, and the source of much later alchemical speculation. The Shebtiw are the source of later stories such as the "Atlantis" myth. They were born in the darkness. They returned to the remnants of a lost world, rebuilding it after the catastrophe. This time they worked in a different manner, not repeating past mistakes, making an organic natural development which was metamorphic, taking remnants that had survived, like old *talatat* bricks, and rebuilding. They also used magick, this is why magick comes into existence. Re-erecting a relic at the water's edge, or reed that survives, the Djeba, so the holy falcon can again alight. They used magick spells, to raise the island and rebuild the primary mansion, on the ruins or remnants of the earlier civilization.

Elsewhere in the account they erect, for the Sun god, another foursquare mandala which lies at the heart of their temple, or this could be another version of the same structure. Now they are guardians, the "Soldiers of Tanen", who was the original Earth god before Geb. They break into four groups to face each of the cardinal directions, making what we might compare to those mandalas famous in esoteric Hinduism.

In this prehistoric version, the Hawk guards to the south accompanied by fourteen companions, also hawks. In the East a serpent called the "Greatly Feared" his fourteen companions also serpents. Similarly in the West, the Bull with fourteen companions and the North, a lion, with fourteen lions.

Only when all these preparations are made when yet another benign Serpent appears in order to deposit eggs in island earth. It reminds me that one of the original cults of Egypt was that of serpents. Traces of these entities are to be found all over later myths, though slightly decentered, they continue to raise their heads in the culture, mostly in peace. One of the locations given for all this is Heliopolis, which is an ancient center that lies beneath modern Cairo. But the myth is generic and applies to any of the sacred centers that together make up Egypt and indeed the whole world. The search for these ancient places began a long time ago but the truth is still out there.

8. The Problem of Evil

A recent study of the building texts from Edfu was undertaken by Kemboly as part of his PhD study (Kemboly 2010). In this he focussed entirely on the origins of evil in Ancient Egypt, exploring the myth of Apophis in all its iterations. He favoured an alternative interpretation to some of these myths, including those of Edfu, although he acknowledged their complexity and multivalent style, and how no one single interpretation is necessary.

As the magick unfolds or allows the new Island-Earth to emerge, several additional supernatural entities appear and make their stand, or rather they squat at the four cardinal directions, each holding an Ankh sign. Of these, eight have lion heads, seven have falcons, seven others have ram's heads, leaving one with an ibis head and one, significant female human figure, wears a seven rayed crown. This later looks like the goddess Sheshat. Sheshat, whose name means "female scribe" is present in her capacity as surveyor and mistress of the built environment. Ever since this mysterious goddess is evoked when scribal/adepts are initiated.

The story says that the divine entities expected the flood at midday, and were there to guard against the return of its chaotic waters. One might ask why midday? It is said that midday is the microcosmic equivalent of the summer solstice. It is part of the fourfold arrangement

Dawn = Equinox (Spring)
Midday = Solstice (Summer)
Sunset = Equinox (Autumn)
Midnight = Solstice (winter)

This arrangement is very important to Egyptian cosmology and there is a magick that flows from it. Rituals to these quarter days are a very hidden aspect of Egyptian religion.

Kemboly thinks this is because at the summer solstice, when sun is most radiant, in these ancient times, the most famous flood, that of the Nile inundation also coincided with the Solstice, as indeed did the other important marker, the heliacal rising of Sirius. All this is known from an astrological monument at Abydos known as the *Book of Nwt*. The book was another of those found on the walls of a sealed room in the famous Osireion, the resurrection chamber, or to give it its Egyptian name, the "hidden place of the underworld".

Also named in this myth is the so-called *Shining one* (hay) which is likely to be another name of the moon. The moon was also viewed as one of the heralds of the inundation, indicating that the Egyptians were well aware that the highest tides occur when the moon and sun were in alignment, or conjunct, which happens on the new moon.

It could be that the primal battle mentioned in all these texts is none other than the inundation, when the waters return, drowning the land, personified later as the god Osiris. Other myths such as that of the two "dividers", Horus and Seth in their lunar avatars, are also involved. It is possible, but somehow, it seems also likely, the Egyptians meant something much more catastrophic. Even if we accept some of this argument that it's linked to the inundation, there is still the fact that the inundation was much more overwhelming, the further back in time one went.

The Nile valley in most of its prehistory was a pretty inhospitable place and could not be successfully settled until the hydraulic balance had calmed down. There must have been several early but abortive attempts to settle that were destroyed or driven out by a seemingly hostile nature. It was indeed a cosmic battle with many episodes until the first successful enterprise took hold.

The myths record this as a primal conflict between the waters and the creator, and this could be the origin of the other conflict motifs in for example the Bible and Plato. Remembering that the conflict was as far as they were concerned, the whole of the known world.

Eventually the Island-Earth was successfully restored, raised up, which is another way of saying, life came to the Nile valley and elsewhere, the flood became a manageable annual event. The first sign that all was well in humanity's new home was the arrival of a falcon. One might think Horus, but this is not the Horus falcon, that comes later. But it could be some sort of precursor or prototype. In anticipation of this happy event, the Submerged Ones (Shebtiw) erected a reed or perch, known as the *Djeba*. The Djeba was a reed but also some kind of unknown relic from the prehistoric times before. So the first nameless falcon flies in and lands on the reed, which is also a relic. The reed is also the scribe's pen.

Now, all this is uncannily like the account of the flood in the Bible, where the "Arkanauts", the dwellers on Noah's ark, receive the first sign that their ordeal is nearly over, when a dove flies to the ark with a reed or remnant of vegetation, which shows them that new life has sprouted somewhere, if they can just find it.

Now I know it is customary for modern skeptics to point out that the Hebrew myths of the Bible are supposedly "appropriated" from the myth cycles of others. But I'd suggest this is really not the way to see it. Hebrew myth is completely entangled with that of the Egyptians, they lived this, it is as much their foundation myth as it is that of the Egyptians. It's even parallel as to how in later but still ancient times, there was a collective debate as to whether the creator god, such as the sungod, was a *unique* entity. And by the way, unique need not mean solitary, a creator can be unique and surrounded by other supernatural entities, usually because they are his progeny. So for example, one talks of Amun as a unique god who became millions of things. Later still, and this is written down as a core doctrine of Hermeticism, which talks of the One (capital O) and the Many.

Incidentally there were no cameras back then with which to record these momentous events, but the next best thing would be to embed things in another magical creation, the alphabet.

As it so happens, the hieroglyph Niwt, O49 in the standard sign list, means generically a village or settlement. But it may actually preserve the original form of this island!

It shows a circular mound crossed by two roads, the archetypal crossroads. One could also consider hieroglyphic sign O47, which shows the prehistoric style of shrine from a primal settlement such as Hierakonpolis, the "citadel of the hawk'.

See also sign O48 for and intermediate form.

This sign is used in the Pyramid texts (Pyr Ut 571 line 1467) - *niwtyw* to signify "those belonging to the lower heaven" or "gods of the undersky" (Allen). These could be those unorganised gods who are able to live after the god Shu has raised the sky for the first time. Raising the sky or raising the submerged island, seems very similar ideas.

So far, the best version of the story I am telling comes from Edfu, in upper Egypt. When people talk, as they sometimes do, of a "hall of records", the mother of them all would be there at Edfu, where documents on this and indeed many other important topics pertaining to Egyptian culture were preserved. It was tantamount to an ancient university.

Edfu's most famous resident was the falcon god Horus, considered to be one of Egypt's original and oldest gods. The current structure, built in what is known as an archaising style that was so popular in the last centuries of Pharaonic culture, when Egypt's rulers were Greek descendents of Alexander the Great's military elite. As we noted several times, Edfu is not too far away from several of Egypt's oldest settlements, including the already mentioned, Hierakonpolis.

Was the falcon god of Hierakonpolis called Horus, or, as seems more likely, was he another, the older falcon deity? There were several to choose from? As it happens the name Horus doesn't even mean Hawk or Falcon, it's literal sense is more of a mask or face, perhaps the mask of god or of heaven.

Here is the hieroglyphic sign :-

Which is vocalized as "Hor" as in Horus

Whereas the hieroglyph for falcon is :-

Which is vocalized as bjk. The Falcon of Hierakonpolis, "citadel of the Hawk", which seems wingless, is written :-

So there was an original falcon god, whose name is mostly unknown but was later called Horus, or whose existence was assimilated to that of Horus, that is to say, a later entity has absorbed the symbolism of the original, Falcon. This is a fairly common process in Egyptian theology, as it is in other evolved religions or belief systems.

The reason the temple scribes at Edfu and elsewhere wrote down these very old legends must have something to do with the fact that the writing was literally "on the wall". Many philosophers of the time could sense that the old pharaonic culture was in its last days. Therefore the wise priests of the temple took any and every opportunity to record in stone, for posterity, the true origins of their culture, which is also the origin of all humanity.

Interesting also is the suggestion that this legend, or *memory*, is connected with the myth of Atlantis. And what is that myth but one of those warnings from history, of how a once mighty culture had fallen because it just wasn't stable enough to withstand the forces of nature.

And where did this myth of Atlantis originate? Not other than from the temple of the goddess Neith at Sais, where it was told to a Greek traveler called Solon. whilst he was visiting this same temple. Manetho (Ma-Netho) the priestly historian whose writings corroborates so many of the otherwise prehistoric accounts, may also have had some connection with this temple.

Perhaps it is no coincidence that the *Hermetica*, classical writings on sacred science, are also linked with this same location, as indeed were many other important issues and debates of the time. It must have been another of those key intellectual hubs that were so important in the classical world.

Solon told the story of Atlantis to his relative Critias, who then told it to Plato, who then committed it to writing in his dialogues, most extensively the *Timaeus*. This particular platonic dialogue is itself closely related to the Hermetic philosophy, and one of the jewels of the Greco-Egyptian world.

Plato may have worked over the myth of Atlantis from sources such as above plus other Greek folklore, tailoring it for his own didactic purposes. To me it looks like yet another garbled version of the narrative we have been discussing from the Edfu temple.

In it we read of how the Greek god: "Poseidon, receiving for his lot an island called Atlantis, begat children by a mortal woman, and settled them in a part of the island, which I will describe...

In this mountain there dwelt one of the earth born primeval men of that country, ... they had an only daughter who was called Cleito (Gift of God). The maiden had already reached womanhood, when her father and mother died; Poseidon fell in love with her and had intercourse with her, ..."

We know from the Edfu myth that *island* could really be referring to the Island-Earth. Poseidon is a very old god, the meaning of whose name is lost in the mists of time. Some authorities say it could mean "earth shaker". He has no exact Egyptian equivalent, some suggest the crocodile god Sobek, or Mesopotamian Yamm or even Noah. The connection of Noah with the Nephilim is explored in a popular movie. Is it another creation myth?

As with all these stories, the original names of the gods have been *inter-translated* for a Greek audience. In the Atlantis myth Poseidon is said to have sired five pairs of twin sons, who ruled his island creation. Five of anything makes more sense in Platonic classification.

A putative Egyptian original would have had four pairs, a very old model of the cosmos, with gods born in pairs. If I had to choose an Egyptian equivalent to Poseidon, it would be Seth-Typhon, who whilst not a god principally of the sea, does have power over it and in some spells battles the god Yamm.

According to the Egyptian underworld *Book of Gates*, (3rd hour) "the trembling centre of the earth, [is] where earthquakes live."

The Egyptian story of the Shebtiw seems archetypal and has much in common with Biblical accounts and indeed similar stories from all over the world. Are we dealing here with a single song-line when one story is continued or copied by another or are these examples of deep mythology and very old magick.

Thus in Aramaic culture, the term *niyphelah* refers to the Constellation of Orion and Nephilim to the offspring of Orion in mythology. (Peake's

Gobekli Tepe, From Wikimedia Commons, the free media repository

commentary on the Bible 1919) Or The *apkallu* of Sumerian mythology who were seven legendary culture heroes from before the Flood. They were of human descent, but possessed extraordinary wisdom which they obtained from the gods. One of the seven apkallu, Adapa, was therefore called "son of Ea" who became a god in Babylon, despite his human origin. Once again the ancient names are simple phonems, words and expressions, which to my mind gives them a very primal expressive quality.

This is what I call deep mythology. It describes

A god called Baal-Seth smiting the Triton

the vast time-line known in geology as the cenozoic or "new life" world. This was the latest in the geological time frame and covers the last 70 million years. This includes the age of the mammals and living beings that emerged in its final millenia. The divine beings are prehistoric and nameless, but traces survive in the earliest of written records. Could it be that written language was developed on the imperative to record all these archaic songlines before the memory faded?

The first beings appear in the Egyptian accounts are ghost-like insubstantial entities, remnants of the what-once-was. The first records of ghosts being from the Pyramid texts. In terms of buildings, it was as if they were vitrified into physical pillars, those used to hold the roof up. Which is very suggestive if you know anything of the pillar entities from Gobekli tepe, who are frozen, in time as if holding up an ancient thatched roof long since gone. Indeed magick connected with the house and home is fairly ubiquitous.

Female Shebtiw?

With these ghosts are other mysterious unknown gods, such as the Shebtiw. Also present are the twins Aa and Wa, who are nominally male, and work together. This issue of twins is a recurring theme in deep mythology. The scribes who recorded these stories treat them as a working duo. The feminine side of the equation is provided by another, originally nameless entity, who has a serpentine form. From the connection or interaction of these two, the Shebtiw and the female serpent, comes a fertilized egg, which is deposited in the island-earth. The symbolism of the Egg from which creation hatched is ubiquitous, whether in later Egyptian myth or indeed wider afield.

Manetho in his fragmentary *Book of Sothis* (Waddell), also mentions a serpent entity, the Agatho-daemon, the founder of Alexandria but in origin Renenutet, the complex serpent deity of pharaonic Egypt. This Agatho-daemon is said to have interpreted and therefore preserved the books of Thoth after the flood.

If one were to ask the Egyptians to specify a precise location for the serpent's nest, they are most likely to say Heliopolis, but this is just one of several *fecund* centres, distributed across the land. Heliopolis is mostly lost, submerged beneath the wonderful, sprawling metropolis of modern Cairo.

Before this new creation, there was a lost world, one that was eventually submerged beneath a colossal flood. This is the time of the "disorganised gods", four generations or groups, who according to yet another text, existed before the god Shu raised the sky onto four pillars. As in the Atlantis myth, and others, the flood occurs in the middle of an ancient battle, indeed may even have been caused by the battle,

or at very least, the great enemy predicted and took advantage of the chaos to press their attack.

In later, literate times, this great adversary was given the name Apophis. But this really is a gloss, a literary spin from the scribes who wrote these accounts and admit they do not really know the name of the original aggressive serpent. They presume he or she to be the ancestor of Apophis and others like them. Which all goes to show we are in the realm of the demonic or "the underworld of the soul". Finite time has begun when, logically, then only can death come into being.

Whatever their names, the character of these entities is always so similar. Thus in the later Greek tradition the serpent is called Typhon which is where we get our modern term for any catastrophic storm, viz a Typhoon.

This moment was envisioned as the building of the first ever temple, first the walls then raising the roof, something reenacted in each subsequent foundation. According to this old narrative from Edfu, the temples of the disorganised time were ruined but never completely destroyed. They endure as submerged remnants, which are still charged and powerful, possessing a residual power, merely dormant, waiting to be reawakened or tapped. Which is how we might continue to use these ancient fragments.

The *Naos of the Decades*. Naos means temple or shrine in Greek. This was a shrine which contained the statue of the god Shu as a lion. The text on this unique monument exposes the cosmic, magical and astrological means to fight the enemies of Egypt. Discovered by the European Intsitute of Underwater Archaeology, directed by Franck Goddio in the waters of East Canopus, Egyptian Delta. (Bomhard 2008)

Being outside of space and time, existing before finite time came into being, they have unlimited, incredible power. Thus it was not surprising that, even in this ruined, latent state, they retain a lot of charge. This charge is just waiting for entities such as "the seven sages" or perhaps "the watchers" to draw upon it, to set it in motion, using it in their new magick, as we also might do.

The sevenfold group of supernatural beings seems to crop up in mythology from all over the world. It looks to me like one of those secrets of the wise that they record at every opportunity. Sometimes they correspond with sevenfold constellations, such as Orion, whose brightest stars are Rigel, Betelgeuse, Bellatrix and Saiph, then, Alnilam and Mintaka of the belt of the Orion. There is image magick connected with this constellation, another remnant, that has long been known by the inhabitants all across the earth.

Another version of the seven can also be the seven stars of the Plough (Ursa major). Yet another is the Pleiades. All these constellations are referenced in ancient monuments, that is to say in buildings. This is one reason why the number seven is always significant in the symbolism, and techniques of magick. Try knocking seven times.

These are just some of the primal patterns that come to us from a nameless aeon. In Egypt this gives rise to arrays or, to make use of a Hindu term, a "mandala" of gods, structured into their original postures, the basic pattern is foursquare, one at each of the cardinal points, then one who takes centre stage, in the middle. Like the great pyramid, which is also a four square monument.

The object known as the *Naos of the Decades*, was used in a similar manner. Naos means temple or shrine in Greek. Usually referring to the cupboard sized holy of holies at the sacred centre of a temple, its beating heart. Decades refers to the images on this particular box, which shows the decans, the ten day periods personified and frozen in time. It was fashioned during the reign of Necktanebo I, where it was part of an assemblage of four similar objects, built to focus battle magick against Egypt's powerful enemies.

This foursquare arrangements now seems so natural an arrangement to us, it has become second nature. We have lived with it so long, remembering the first times the land rose up and the chaotic water receded, the foundation of a lost building is revealed, the first temple of the beginning times, on whose ruins another may be raised. This is the first house or mansion for the gods. We always remember it, even when we don't.

And although those ancient ones will never live or rule again, things can never be the same, they continue some form of revived existence, memorialized in all buildings that come after, or that have been raised on those same symbolic foundations. In magick we remember them, unconsciously repeating these patterns, until the role playing becomes real.

So, to repeat, the Nephilim of the Bible seem to be the same class of entities encountered in Egyptian records. To use a literary metaphor they are "Those who must be kept". They are in their temples, the younger ones above ground, the older ones beneath the floor, in the foundations, which can be accessed by those who have the key. Which reminds me of an account of the Kabbalah from Henry Corbin, who says, when the temple of Jerusalem was about to be destroyed by the Babylonians, they handed back the keys to the angels.

An Adept is one who knows these hidden ways, the sealed crypts and chambers, whether real or metaphorical, which even now are often still discoverable. The power *beneath* has a big influence in our mundane world for those who choose to make use of it, for this is one of the powers, the "baraka" wielded in magick – which the Egyptians called Heka.

One of the first acts executed by the magician, often subconsciously, is the duplication, mostly in the imaginal realms, of the raising of the first house. Ultimately this comes from Egypt but because of the convoluted history of magick and religion, over many centuries, millenia even, that have elapsed, these origins have become obscured by the other mythologies through which the doctrine has been filtered. Or perhaps we should acknowledge that magick is very practical and often focussed on the mundane, things like making, maintaining and protecting a house. See for example some of the methods of Chinese Magic in Jason Read's translation of the classic grimoire of folk magick that is the *Luban* (2023).

The Egyptians had a way of embedding this memory of place within the scribal caste, one assumes from whom the adepts were drawn. Every major temple had a working space called "The House of Life". Principally this is to store all the paper copies of the very many books and texts that were inscribed on the coffins, tomb, and temple walls. There has to be a temple library, where all the special books were kept, and studied, copies made etc. Sometimes the House of Life is very small, just enough space for shelves and rolled up manuscripts. Larger institutions have much bigger facilities where no doubt scribes could be trained and do their work.

What interests me is how, just as in modern libraries, the great one's at least, the arrangement of sources replicates the opening setup of the nameless gods described earlier. It's a kind of theatre of memory or knowledge – also called mimesis, to imitate or mime. Which as anyone will tell you is one of the tricks of ancient gnosis, associating a memory with a place.

It might be that you want to go further, to play out in the actual performance of magick? It could all be about role playing. A complex thing, but the magician also plays the role, or work of the gods, literally a theurgy. Whenever he or she starts the magick, they almost always orientate themselves as if in a square house, just like in the beginnings, we have been exploring. You the reader may be already doing this, or if not soon will.

In your mind you start at the centre, where stands the hidden god who is none other than you, the magician. They could also be the buried one. They proceed by invoking the four directions, north, south, east, west, and of course the above and below. In this simple thought, which is an act of magick, one is emulating the gods, the important ones at least, in that very first temple.

Now you are ready to learn other things in this space. What did those ancient giants do next? They extrapolated the temple outwards. I'm reminding you that essentially, they built a school, in which they then taught astronomy, the science of the heavens and magic to humans.

Do you remember the first spaces and buildings in which you learnt things that have stayed with you throughout your life so far. In antiquity, Egypt, was even called the temple of the world, but perhaps it is also an academy or university.

9. The Underworld of the Soul

So how did the Egyptians connect with this underworld of the soul? And how might we emulate them? How it is made a lived reality in one's spiritual or magical work? Consider the well preserved examples of temples in Egypt, these can be explored, in part physically but then metaphysically via imagination and dreams. There are many structures that lend themselves to this approach but for now I offer two of the best preserved examples. The Osireion or "Cenotaph" of Sety I at Abydos, which is particularly important for the whole long history of magick and also for the practice known later as "alchemy". Many core principles of the latter cannot be distinguished from, and are often synonymous with magick.

Another would be the Apet temple, a shrine to the mother of Osiris-Amun attached to the temple of the moon god Khonsu at Karnak. Research shows this to have been a centre for a mystery cult that played an important role in the training and initiation of adepts in the late classical world. It also has a secret subterranean chamber which was the home of a symbolic giant.

The Osireion

Despite appearances, this structure seems to have been built at the same time as the main temple above it. Some of its walls act as bulwark supporting and preventing the layer of sand that lies beneath the temple, which otherwise would have subsided with disastrous consequences. The finished structure, buried beneath a vast dome of earth, was shaded by six trees. Archaeologists were able to identify one tree as Tamarisk, in the remains of the tree-pits. All of these features have significance, much of which is lost to us now, although details can be reclaimed given careful, immersive study.

The entrance to this structure begins from outside the temenos, which signals a mystery cult. Such "private" entrances are a feature that can also be seen at the Apet, and is one of the first clues to the structures "extra curricular use" outside of standard temple routine. Remembering that temples, being the house of the gods, were closed at night, the model is a domestic routine, the gods need their time out etc.

There is an ancient robber's tunnel that led from a corner of the Osireion to another sealed room in the temple proper. The robbers were obviously

VIEW LOOKING NORTH-EAST FROM THE CENTRE OF THE WEST WALL OF THE INNER OSIRIS HALL

View of the Inner Osiris Complex, The Temple of King Sethos I at Abydos, edited by Alan H. Gardiner, and largely devoted to the superb and beautiful copies of the wall paintings of the temple done by Ms. Amice Calverley. The blocked chamber would be through the doorway into the Isis chamber and behind its northern wall. It lies wedged between two chapels of Horus, and this arrangement maybe significant.

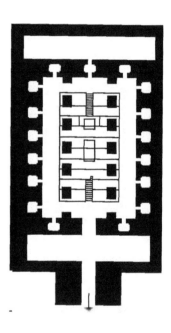

"Strabo's Well" and the Tomb of Osiris, drawing by Edouard Naville. In classical times this site was known as Strabo's well after the account of the roman traveller's visit to the powerful natural underground spring. The entrance was from the bottom left, the northern side (local) then one turns due East to face the central axis of the chamber.

intrigued by another "sealed room" but never got far before being overwhelmed by subsidence from the layer of sand that underpins the whole structure. It does show how even in antiquity the temple complex really was a place of mystery, patrolled at night by unseen forces, often thought to be demonic, which is a catchall for beyond one's pay grade.

The symbolic entrance through the temenos mentioned above was bricked up soon after construction. Entrance was only possible via a collapsed section of the same tunnel. This was the regular entrance for many years. I'd argue that this heterodox, *ad hoc* way in, could be intentional, because it was psychologically unsettling, and thus added to the sense of wonder.

The main entrance passage bears on its western side a version of *The Book of Gates*, facing this from the east are various mythological underworld figures. At the end of the sloping passageway is an enlarged section which seems to be a space to allow for a 90 degree turn to face the main axis of the room, which would be necessary if one were trying to manoeuvre a large Egyptian stone coffin into the main shrine. This might also serve as a mustering point before progressing into the complex.

King Sety was destined to be buried in his magnificent tomb in the Valley of the Kings, 100 miles 160km further north. It was rather a clear signal that

when thinking oneself into this sacred space one has to change one's trajectory from North-South, the direction of the entrance tunnel, making a turn to the symbolic West-East. All of this was magical significant, or as we would say nowadays, psychologically important. Diana Kreikamp, in her study of the *Amduat*, has done a good job of decoding the various shifts of direction inherent in the underworld books:-

The complete version of the Amduat unfolds on the four walls around the sarcophagus. This results in the King lying literally in the middle of the Duat. The ellipse shape of the chamber divides the Duat in four cardinal directions; North, East, South and West. The head of the sarcophagus is facing North, so the feet point towards the South. In this position the King gazes upon the Fifth and the Twelfth Hour that are depicted next to each other. This is a very befitting position for the King since these two hours signify the beginning of the transformation process and the final rebirth.

The route of the Sungod through the twelve hours is quite interesting since every hour takes place in a specific cardinal direction. The text of the *Amduat* clearly explains in which specific cardinal direction an hour has to be depicted on the wall in the hidden chamber (i.e. burial chamber). These instructions can be found in the introductory text of each hour. Due to these instructions, the hours do not seem to be depicted in a chronological order on the walls. However, since the Sungod jumps from one cardinal direction to another, he does travel through the hours in a chronological order. (Kreikamp 2021 : 18)

The main chamber at Abydos is a single room roofed with megalithic beams to give the pitched-roof look so important to Egyptian religious ideology. The central hall, which was never completely finished, consists of an island surrounded by a channel. The pitched stone roof was to be held up by ten great pillars of rose granite, still in situ, and of which we can see seven are monoliths.

The central island, surrounded by living waters, has two stairways, one of 12 the other of 11 steps that lead down into the water channel. On the island itself there were two cavities, one square that looks to be for the canopic jars. The second, oblong shaped cavities looks to be where a sarcophagus, presumably of Osiris, might rest.

Becoming a Giant

Ritual texts tell us Osiris was buried in stages, often separated by long periods of time, perhaps allowing 12 months of incubation. This echoes his double murder by Seth, his demonic initiator, who first drowns him in the living waters. This waters are a key feature of the structure which is designed to take advantage

Enigmatic composition from ceiling of corridor G in tomb of Ramses VI, Valley of Kings. Giant talismanic image of Sun and Moon to prevent intrusive spirits from entering at magical weak point in the construction where two separate tunnels are perilously close. (Darnell 1995)

of a natural aquifer. This immersion in waters was a key component of several related magical processes, starting perhaps with mummification. But then we find the idea of a sacred bath of rejuvenations recurs on specifically alchemical texts of all times. It is a key mystery. We can replicate a little of this via use of sacred baths (See *Aromagick*). But the process does not end there.

The loyal followers of Osiris eventually recovered his drowned corpse and set about trying to reanimate it. But Seth again intervenes, this time dismembering the corpse into a significant number of parts, one of which, the head, is preserved and memorialized at Abydos. The ritual involves rememberment of the corpse, with special attention being devoted to the phallic region, which has actually been eaten by Seth, who does so, taking on the form of a cat-fish. Secret rites are connected with the return of the phallus.

It has to be said that the Egyptian corpse has wider connotations than what we moderns know. It is the raw material, a potential, waiting to be molded anew. Consider this from the *Book of Earth : The Creation of the Solar Disk* (Roberson 2012).

> Entering the corpse that is the Nun,
> In it are more corpses
> Those of the two goddesses,
> Amunet in the west, Atenet in the east

Another enigmatic, protective image from Tomb of Ramses VI, showing figure with solar head and serpentine feet, precursor of Abrasax of later times. (Darnell 1995)

Together they are with this great god,
The one who also traverses the land of the dead,
Which is Dark-of-Heart,
Which is in the hidden chamber:

In the Apet sanctuary discussed below, it is the God Ra who returns this power. The union of Nocturnal Sun and Lord of the Dead being a key mystery here too. There is certainly a sexual resonance involved, and one that the Egyptian would express with no fear of the homoerotic implications. Sexual undertones are always part of the alchemical world view.

In all we see the process of later times in proto perhaps strongest form here, the solve and coagula. The process is also specifically called *becoming a giant*. Thus the final resting place of the reconstituted Osiris is a second, colossal, burial chamber in the Osireion. This was a transverse chamber, running North-South, at the top of the illustration. This chamber has three texts devoted to the giant star-goddess Nwt, who amongst other things is the personification of the Milky Way, which, coincidentally also runs North-South.

The Giant and the Dwarf

The presence of giants in Egyptian visual culture is easily overlooked and significance un-interpreted. For example in corridor G of the tomb of Ramses VI, a distant relative of Sety I, there is a significant protective image. Placed where adjustments to the tomb design generated a sloping ceiling just before the entrance to the main chamber. This was considered a weakpoint in the design due to the closeness of the tunnels of Ramses VI with that of an earlier tomb. So a point of egress for spirits that need to be sealed magically.

At this point the scene shows a giant sun and moon conjoined or perhaps a double sun. Not too far away comes another intensely magical image, the precursor of the giant Abraxas, surrounded by the so-called enigmatic text, a code used by the Egyptian to preserve the deepest of their mysteries.

Similarly this being is synonymous the "The Giant cosmos spanning stature that Re-Osiris assumes at the moment of his emergence from the easter horizon" (Roberson BOE 2012 31). There is another version of this same gigantic figure from Golden Shrine of Tutankamun. "He who hides the hours" . (see page 48 above to remind yourself how this image looks).

The walls of the giant sarcophagus chamber at Abydos, were the only ones actually finished in Sety's lifetime. This must be because they gave context to all of the preparations for death and rebirth. Thus they have been called "The Primary Corpus" – ie the key texts that we all must study. Placed on the eastern side of the vaulted ceiling, which is in an archaic style of the pyramid age, is the remarkable "Book of Nwt" or, to give it its Egyptian title: *Book of Fundamentals of the stars*. Nwt, is seen here as another giant figure, as she is often shown elsewhere, for example Dendara, as the largest divine representation in all of Egypt. No temple is dedicated to her alone, unless you count this as one. She is part of every temple, in this sense she is ubiquitous.

Additional texts of the primary corpus follow, including the so-called "Dramatic Text of Nwt", and the instructions for a Shadow Clock. Time and its passage is key to these spiritual operations. The other half of the roof of the Osireion, to the west, has the "Book of Night" showing the resuscitation of King Sety by Nwt. In effect this would apply to any human accompanying Ra-Osiris through the stages or hours of the night. This magick involves us in some psycho-somatic gesture, emulating the process of dissolution, then reconstitution. Dissolving and coagulating, in parallel to the Nocturnal Sun (Ra) and Lord of the Dead (Osiris). The process is so secret it was written in ancient code.

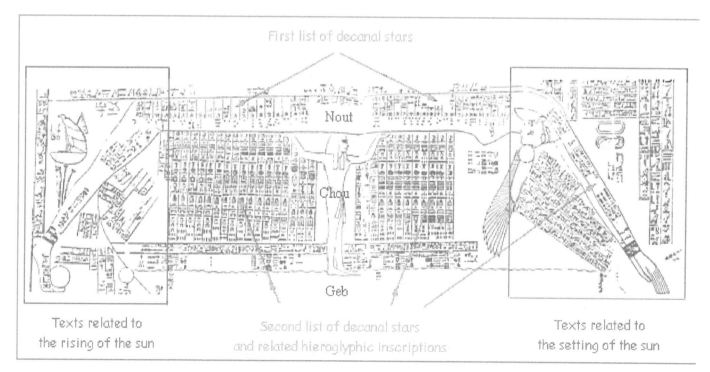

Drawing of "The Book of Nwt" from the Osireion at Abydos

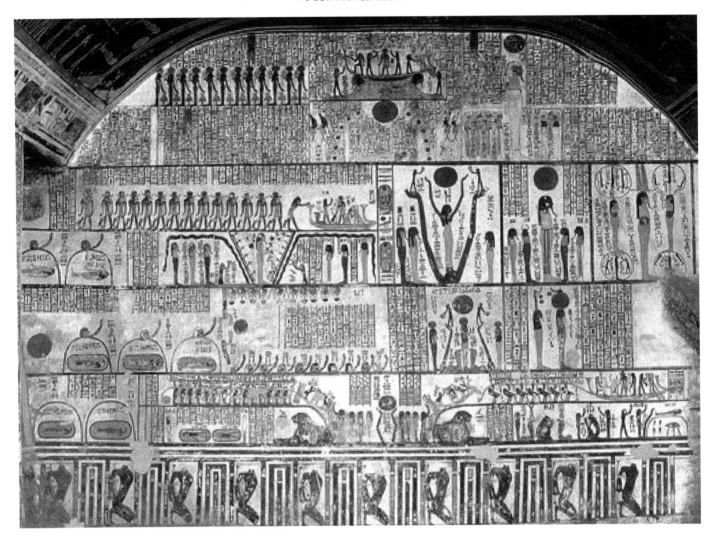

The West wall of the Tomb of Ramses VI showing *Book of Earth*. Forming one axis of the "primary corpus" around the person in the sarcophagus

In other monuments the "Book of Night" is paired with the "Book of Day", one of best examples being the domed sarcophagus chamber of Ramses VI. The domed shape there was intentional, and is a development of the pitched roofs of the Osireion and older examples. Here at the Ramses VI monument we get a clearer idea of how the "primary corpus" forms a complete horizon around the deceased in their coffin. The *Books of Day* and *Books of Night* above making the North/South Axis, the *Books of the Earth* to the North and South walls, making the East/West Axis.

This whole underground assemblage at Abydos was used long after its original intention was changed or forgotten. In the work of Strabo, a Greek historian and traveler in Egypt, the powerful internal spring is viewed as a well within a grove of Egyptian Acanthus. This grove replaced an original of six tamarisk trees, wood from which was discovered by archaeologists. What persists overtime was the grove-like structure.

In later times the place had quite a reputation, as the site of a famous oracle shrine for the "typhonian" god Bes, a demonic protector or perhaps another initiator of Osiris. Zosimus the famous alchemist knew it and seems to have referenced its mysteries in his books of alchemy. It was a spirited place even for those priests charged with the overseeing, causing them to leave messages seeking protection from some of the troublesome demons there:

"Adoration of Ra horakht, lord of the two lands, the great god, king of gods, lord of horns, with pointed atef crown … king … may he save the scribe … from the demons that are in this place. May he save the scribe Pedamun from the demons that are in this place." (Frankfort 1925)

Coptic Christians, who later reused the site as a church, but not before the obligatory exorcism of Bes, as claimed in the Hagiography of Moses of Abydos, concerned by Coptic Nuns visits to the local "demon" called Bes.

Dreaming is the common ground between the Bes oracle and the Egyptian alchemical tradition. Dreaming, whilst awake and asleep was and is, a big part of early alchemical instructional texts.

Intriguingly, no images of Bes have been found in the Osireion, though a pierce of apotropaic graffiti there mentioned a class of demons, the *hatyw*, the word spelt with a determinative sign of a flint armed monkey god.

There are three known spells connected to the Bes oracle. The prototype comes from venerable New Kingdom *Papyrus Harris*, for protection of Osiris by a dwarf god, assume Bes. (Frankfurter 1997).

Oh Dwarf here of heaven, the great dwarf whose

head is large, whose back is long, whose thighs are short, the great support that extends unto the Underworld, the lord of the great corpse, which rests in Heliopolis, the great living god who rests in Busiris! Pay attention to NN born of NN! Guard him by night and protect him like you protected Osiris from Him-with-the-hidden-name on that day of the burial in Heliopolis. (P Harris 8.5-9.5, tr Borghouts, Ancient Egyptian Magical Texts 1978 : 90)

The Oracle is attested before the Roman era, and is therefore parallel with the development of Serapis oracle at same site.

How did it all work? Many came to the Bes oracle seeking to excel, a great many athletes and young people, often with their families. Makes me think the

Bes alongside Tutu, two demonic, "typhonian" type gods of later times.

quest for resurrection or is it resurgence, is the goal of the young. The charismatic dwarf, and before him the wounded, Osiris is the one to ask. Probably based in the Osiris cellar of the temple of Seti at Abydos.. These hidden chambers (cella) in the main temple are located above the underground crypts of the Osireion. Much of the passage to the underworld chamber here must have been astral stuff. Or maybe just knowing the existence of this black box and hidden room, was evocative enough for those sleeping above it.

Here is PGM VIII 64-110, one of the three extant spells of later times that facilitate this process:

Request for a dream oracle of Besa

On your left hand draw Besa in the way shown to you below.

Put around your hand a black cloth of Isis and go to sleep without giving answer to anyone. The remainder of the cloth hang loosely around your neck.

This is the ink with which your draw. (In practice red ink does the trick) Blood of a crow, blood of a white dove, lumps of incense, myrrh, black writing ink, cinnabar, sap of mulberry tree, rain water, juice of a single stemmed wormwood and vetch. With this write:

Prayer to him toward the setting sun:
"Borne on the breezes of the wand'ring winds,
Golden-haired Helios who wields the flame's
Untiring light, who drives in lofty turns
Around the great pole; who create all things

Yourself which you again reduce to nothing.
For from you come the elements arranged
By your own laws which cause the whole world
through its four yearly points rotating.

If you go to the depths of earth and reach
The region of the dead [and dread],
send up the truthful Prophet
out of that innermost abode to [teach].

I beg you
LAMPSOUêR SOUMARTA BARIBAS
DARDALAM PHORBêX,
lord, send forth your holy daimon
ANOUTH ANOUTH (Osiris, Osiris)
SALBANACHAMBRê BRêITH,
immediately, immediately;

quickly, quickly;

in this night, come.”

If you wish to call him for a direct vision take a strip of linen, soak it in sesame oil you have mixed with cinnabar, and place the linen as a wick in a lamp that is not coloured red. The lamp should be lighted with sesame oil. Place it opposite you, say the formula and he will come to you. Have near you a small tablet so that you may write as much as he says, lest after going to sleep you forget.

“I call upon you the headless god, having your face beside your feet, the one who hurls lightning and thunders; you are the one whose mouth is continually full of fire, the one placed over Necessity. I call upon you, the god placed over Necessity.

iaeô sabaôth adônai zabarbathiaô;

you are the one lying on a coffin of myrrh having resin and bitumen as an elbow cushion, the one who they call ANOUTH ANOUTH. Rise up, daimon, You are not a daimon, but the blood of the two falcons who chatter and watch before the head of Osiris. You are the oracle-giving god SALBANACHAMBRê ANOUTH ANOUTH sabaôth adônai iê ie iê ie” (add the usual as you wish).

Go to sleep on a rush mat, having an unbaked brick beside your head.

What you draw is of this sort: A naked man, standing, having a diadem on his head, and in his right hand a sword that by means of a bent (arm) rests on his neck, and in the left hand a wand. If he reveals to you, wipe off you hand wih rose perfume. [figure]”

The existence of dream incubation for *private individuals* can’t be proved before the late period of the above spell which also is when the oracle at Abydos flourished. Dreams were however part of earlier funeral rites, where it was perhaps a priestly or initiated duty. The subtle difference here is that its not for ordinary individuals, but exclusively for the Pharaoh and his immediate family. For them it seems that sleeping in the temple was always something they did. There is said to be no record that sleeping there was for the purpose of experiencing a dream. There may have been other reasons, such as the sanctity of the place, that were the primary purpose. So there were visits to temples, that would be followed by a dream but maybe this was later, after returning home. Being very pedantic, this doesn’t fit the standard model where the dream and the temple visit have to coincide. However, for me, the existence of New Kingdom dream manuals makes it very likely it was an earlier practice, even if strictly speaking, the connection cannot be proven. (Kasia Szpakowski *Behind Closed Eyes*). For practical recommendation to try any of these techniques for yourself, contact the author.

10. The Apet
and the Ancestors under the Floor

Let's consider a sacred space known as the Apet, which is a shrine within the immense ritual enclosure that is Karnak. One immediate clue to the specialness of this structure is the fact that it has its own dedicated entrance. This provided a way for initiates and celebrants through the sacred boundary wall or temenos. Otherwise the main entry to the Karnak is via the monumental pylon gates. The Apet has its own entrance that nevertheless shares the same East West orientation.

The eminent Egyptologist Claude Traunecker worked on the site for many years, and was able to make several new discoveries. Many of these were in the subterranean crypts, otherwise strictly off limits. De Wit's original 1958 survey omitted the crypts it is reported due to snake infestation. The same has been passed down ever since, also the once offlimits shrine is now renovated and open to the public.

We can now safely follow in the footsteps of the ancients, passing through the well preserved monumental doorway. Here we encounter an altar set before the goddess Sekhmet, remains of whose statue is sited directly on one's path into the temple. The convenient horned altar was plainly designed for the pilgrim to make an offering, which was like a portion of animal flesh, burnt to ashes on the altar.

Beyond this is by Egyptian standards, a modest temple, the product of Ptolemaic times. This was in turn built over the remains of an earlier edifice, built by King Taharqa of Kush, in what is now Sudan. 1070 BCE −591 BCE. He was a king of the Nubian dynasty that conquered Egypt.

Inside the first, mostly destroyed courtyard, the faithful would have encountered a healing shrine, now lost, but probably of Horus. It was a place of purification but also where water could be passed over a statue of the god. This was collected in a convenient basin and imbibed as a healing and protective fluid.

Other nearby features, would have included the now lost ruins of a *Komasterion* for the temple, i.e. a place of assembly of the priests, including storage

The narrow passageway between the temple of moon god Khonsu and the Apet sanctuary. The door leads to the crypt where mysteries were celebrated. Either side of the door are show the representative of the regions, each bearing their local products, including Seth bringing the wine of the oasis.

rooms for offerings. In the traumatic Ptolemaic dynasties, a lot of dramas played out at Karnak, including an ancient scandal to do with embezzlement of temple funds. The Kamasterion also acted as a chancery for money, and coincidentally a large cache of bronze coins was found in its ruins.

The remaining temple proper has a unique design, a true spiritual "black box", fifteen meters square. Serge Sauneron called it, metaphorical, "nuclear generator".

It has a threefold arrangement, the central path leads to the holy of holies, the left-hand shrine (north) concerns the resurrection of Osiris, the right-hand shrine, the Birth of Horus & recognition of his relationship with the god Amun. There are several crypts that were accessed by sliding flagstones. These had lots of different functions aside from the side chapels North and South, there are corresponding long corridor-like rooms to each of the side chapels that are accessed independently but are related, sharing the same extraordinary iconography. Beneath each side chapel are long crypts or basements, themselves approximately 10 kilometers long. No snakes, but what did they house? Here were lost masterpieces of Egyptian art, giant statues of Osiris. They were gilded metal, which in itself is one of the key mysteries of Egypt, the interplay between copper and gold, which later becomes the alchemical tradition. Osiris, shown as a giant, hidden in the crypt, is another feature whose significance it would be difficult to overplay.

One can surmise that all these great mysteries were revealed to silent initiates at key moments in a secret priestly cult. This temple abounds in anomalies in style, many of which were bound to have provoked wonder and *gnosis* in the candidate, as these things were revealed.

Though other temples in the area have crypts, very few have surviving decoration. And the previously unknown images in the Northern crypt set out an important theological notion of the connection between the cult of Amun and Osiris here called Onnophris (wnn-nfr) meaning "perfect one". This union of Osiris, Lord of the Dead, and Amun-Re as Nocturnal Sun, in one giant figure, ever one of the seminal mysteries of Egyptian religion.

The crypt beneath the inner holy of holies in the central shine, would likely have served as a symbolic tomb of Osiris, another Osireion. It was also the final resting place of the giant of gold, and the power source, a spiritual battery on which the adepts of the temple could draw. And given the centrality of the living statues in Egyptian magick, one might speculate on the ancient methods used to turn them on.

On this we have the text of one of Egypt's most potent rituals, that of "Opening the Mouth" performed on statues and other ritual objects, including the temple itself. This rite, begun at the temple workshops, culminated in a material and psycho-physical process whose deep significance we can only guess at, at the same time as we try to rediscover how it was done. Physical presence to these objects and decorations, loaded as they are with lines from the primary corpus of books, must be considered the way it was done. With all things in place, the adept could enter a deep, psycho-physical trance, in which they were enabled to rebirth themselves. To know more, then join us in our quest to recover these ancient methods.

11. Conclusion

The Nephilim was usually considered to be a purely Jewish concept. However, given what we now know about the Egyptian sources, it is entirely credible, I'd say proven that it is actually deeply shared myth. We discovered how crucial the giant is in Egyptian religious thought; a fact easily overlooked.

The Egyptian equivalents of the Nephilim are central to the mechanics of its ancient magical practice. Giants such as Osiris regularly appear in the so-called underworld books, such as the *Amduat* and *Book of Earth*. The star-goddess Nwt is view as another giant, and is physically the largest figure represented in Egyptian temples, where her image, for example at Denderah, occupies entire ceilings.

Consider also the phenomena of foundation deposites, standard in the construction of temples, palaces, tombs, and forts. These were placed at the corners of buildings or at points of importance in the structure. Deposits were also placed under obelisks, columns, hypostyle halls, sanctuaries and along the central axes of the building. These join other objects under the floor, decommissioned statues and previous foundations. This is all part of the mindset whereby the old ones, giants from the previous creation, are also envisioned as lying under the foundations of the building. This was both an imaginal thing but, as we see in some Ptolemaic buildings such as the Apet, the empty crypts once contained oversize statues of copper and gold. These were magical substances, central to the process we call alchemy. For the Egyptian, the process of rebirth, and recreation of substances, was modelled on the birth process itself. That is to say, the birth process, which was always mysterious, was the model for the transformation of all substances.

We do not have all the parts but we can see where we must go. The core elements are orientation to the cardinal points. The construction of an idealised house for these entities, a real place that assists us in the mental task of bringing this to life in the inner realm. To do this, we must literally call them to mind.

Appendix: The Horoi

1. Halves of the signs in the circle of (zodiacal) constellations are called by the name of their series Horas. I will describe them briefly, but in detail, together with their various shapes, insignia, distinguishing marks, and forms.

2. The first Hora in Aries wears red clothes and is flaming like the Sun at Doomsday. He holds a sword and a firebrand in his hands. Half of his hair is tawny, and his ear-rings are of gold. He is a fierce man who has raised the staff of Death for the sake of protection.

3. This is a man-shaped creature whose cry is loud and who has a long, thin face. Standing in the midst of flocks of goats and sheep, and mounted on a goat, he rules his host.

4. The second Hora in Aries wears a garland of skulls. His bow blazes with arrows. He has the strength of an elephant. He is bound with a half girdle, and his clothes are black. His limbs are adorned with snakes. Bearing a sword and (elephant's) skin, and of terrible figure, he wears the diadem (of Siva).

5. Entering the forest with his swift thieves, he lets loose destruction, this fearful-faced man, splitting open the highest peak with his bolts. He thinks of destruction and ruin (?).

6. The first Hora in Taurus is a woman who carries a pitcher of cow's milk and clarified butter. She is pre-eminent, rising up with an axe in her hand. Her face is like that of a horse. She plays and swings gracefully, wear ing bright-coloured robes, and her feet tinkle with anklets.

7. She is four-footed. Girdle-strings surround her body. She is filled with thirst, and is fond of all sorts of food. She is beautiful with her heavy breasts, has handsome hips, and wears a bright, pendant girdle.

8. The second Hora in Taurus is a youthful woman with pleasing eyes. She is intelligent, and pale with the beauty of campaka-flowers. She knows the rules of sciences, pharmacology, and the arts. She is adorned with garments of silk, this blazing one.

9. She appears in an assembly of farmers, sacrificing her body to Brahma (?) like a woman in childbirth. She has garlands, perfumes, and cosmetic powders. Drunk on draughts of soma-juice, she speaks in a lovely voice.

10. The first Hora in the third sign holds a lyre in his hand. His complexion is the colour of a parrot's tail-

feather. He is an artistic man whose clothes hang loosely and whose nature it is to love singing, dancing, and listening (to music). Seated on a cane chair he composes poetry.

11. He runs after women and is clever in love. His sides are bound in the embrace of a maiden's arms. He is not much of a businessman, but he is a destroyer of gentleness and beauty, a very reprehensible person.

12. The second Hora in the third sign is established as being a woman whose actions are charming and glowing with youth. She is pale and red limbed, clever and grateful. She is besieged by the leader of an army in a wide-spreading war. Clothed in red, she wears a dangling red necklace.

13. Raising her arms, she cries out when she is robbed. She is made naked by thieves in a park, but is brought back by means of an armed conflict.

14. The first Hora in the fourth sign is a woman who holds a blossoming lotus in her hand. She stands in the water, pale as the colour of a campaka flower. Her upper-garment and ornaments are pale like moon-beams. Her limbs are adorned with the splendour of full and half necklaces.

15. Leaning on the branch of an asoka-tree in a garden, she recalls to mind her beloved. Her necklace trembles on her girdle and breasts.

16. The second Hora in the fourth sign is established as being a very pale man in the middle of a garden who seizes bright weapons and who has a neck like a horse's. He is a lover whose radiance is made beautiful by playful glances. Holding a lotus, the beloved one pours forth his complaints.

17. He wears variegated garments and ornaments at Doomsday (?). The ointment on his body is as bright as Cupid's. He is remembered....

18. The first Hora in Leo is to be spoken of as a bold man whose form is as terrible as a lion's. He is blazing and fierce-the restrainer of change. He has upward-curving tusks, and is like Yama and Kala. He stands in the midst of battles between Nisadas and thieves.

19. He has bound on his quiver. Desiring to taste flavours, he slays (?) deer in mountain caves. His teeth are like those of the lord of elephants. His firm chest is wounded.

20. The second Hora in the house of the Sun is a fierce man who delights in battle. His bow is drawn back; his garment is a deer-skin. He is a eunuch, but, bearing his armour of gold, he protects women. The hair on his body is long.

21. He is bald-headed and gat-toothed. Impassioned, he touches the genitals of a man or a woman. Together

with the robbers of his band he shouts terribly and shrilly in the desert.

22. The first Hora in the sixth sign is a black and white woman who is charming and wise. She is wet with her menstruation and has filthy garments. She thinks of fine clothes, and, desiring a son, has intercourse with the man she loves.

23. She cries in the forest among the serving-girls of Brahma (?), leaning on a branch that is in full fruit and leaf. She is in distress and without money, and her body is stretched out. She has attained beauty.

24. The second Hora in Virgo is said to be a man pale as moon-beams who knows how to write. He wears a beautiful and spotless garland of blossoming lotuses. He is handsome with teeth as bright as the rays of the Moon.

25. He is remembered ... He adores his beloved. A pleasing man, he is eloquent and clever in crafts, dances, and the weaving of garlands, as well as in the use of a needle.

26. The first Hora in Libra is a man who is black and white. He is clever and knows spells .... He carries a pair of scales, and is steadfast in the five duties.

27. Standing within the market-place, he wears a bright and handsome garland. He is in control of grain, etc., and of all sorts of coins. His seal, consisting of a dart,

a sword, and an arrow, is accepted, and he observes a vow without limit.

28. The second Hora in Libra is one who is accustomed to pitiless and manly deeds. He has prominent teeth. Hating the accomplishment of protection, he carries bright-coloured arrows, a knife, and a drawn sword (with which to assail his enemies).

29. He is a smasher of houses whose seal is an injury to others. His hair is erect, and like a blanket. Crying aloud in the market-place, he jingles a bell and causes fright among the people.

30. The first Hora in the eighth sign is a man of terrible form-blazing, fierce, and most dreadful. He delights in injury, and wears a garland of gold. Yearning for battle, he dons his armour which is bound with serpents.

31. He has prominent teeth and is violent like Death. His limbs and his eyes are red, his hair like numerous swords. He slays living creatures with poison and a sword like Mahesvara angry at Doomsday.

32. The second Hora in the eighth sign is a level-standing (?) woman with a black body who has poisonous mouth and hands. She is the cause of (the use of) weapons, battles, diseases, and dangers, as she makes her snakes swell, writhe, and sway.

33. Her neck is clung to by great serpents proud of their poisonous breath. Her girdle consists of strings

of jewels. She is filled with anger, and her teeth are flashing and fearful. Biting her lower lip, she creates tumult and quarrels.

34. The first Hora in Sagittarius is a man whose bow is drawn to the limit. He wears the Moon in his diadem, and is moon-faced. His hair is bound with gold. He races with his horse, this protector of the sacrifice.

35. He stands in penance in the forest of asceticism and on the peaks of mountains, slaying the race of the Dasyus. He knows the proper use of each element of the Vedas and the sacrifice, and accomplishes all his desires. His eyes are as wide as lotuses.

36. The second Hora in Sagittarius is a woman of handsome brilliance who is full of motion, pride, and playfulness, and who shines like gold. She understands magic, is artful in (the use of) poison and weapons, and gives clever advice.

37. Seated on an auspicious throne she looks at an excellent casket filled with jewels and other riches. With spotless ointment on her body as she gazes at the jewels from the sea, she shines like Laksmi with splendour.

38. The first Hora in Capricorn is a man with jagged teeth who is hideous and fierce, armed with a club like Death at Doomsday. He breaks the peace, this wearer of a deer-skin.

39. He guards his iron, his slaves, and his buffaloes, and, standing in the water, defends his black grain. Letting loose the rough thieves who are devoted to him, he bears (the attack of) the Mlecchas (barbarians) and the chief Candalas.

40. The second Hora in Capricorn is a woman with loose hair who has a red face and red arms and who stands on one foot; they say that the rest of her is black. Her belly hangs down, and her teeth are dreadful like a crocodile's.

41. She shines with blue unguents, and her limbs are covered with garments. Brightly coloured, she is adorned with ornaments made of the metal of the Pisacas. Entering the water and standing at Mare's Mouth (the Entrance to Hell), she (raises ?) her voice again and again.

42. The first Hora in Aquarius is a man who glistens with black unguents. His teeth are dreadful. He is black, and wears the beauty of a skin....

43. He knows many desired arts, and his hands are employed in many crafts. A pot is on his shoulders. His thoughts are covetous; he is a suitable leader of those whose emblem is a pot. His hands hold dice for gambling. He is beloved as one who desires to defend (his friends).

44. The second Hora in Aquarius is remembered to be a woman adorned with silken garments. Her robes are

black, and her hand grasps a noose. Her eyes are as wide as a lotus. She is learned in the sacred texts.

45. Her body is tall and black, her hair reddish and wild. She is by nature clever. Being in the final stage of intoxication and surrounded by throngs of Water-Rakasis, she restrains Fate together with the Night of Doom.

46. The first Hora in Pisces is an excellent lady who is loved by one who has crossed over (the ocean). Standing on a path beside the Great Sea, she is shining and moon-faced. Her laughter causes a trembling and a graceful movement of her arms and breasts.

47. Surrounded by women who are pleasing in every way and who have risen up from the shore of the Great Sea, she shines forth, her limbs adorned with red garments. She accomplishes all her objectives, and is without misfortune.

48. The second Hora in Pisces is said to be a woman wearing ear-rings made of the superior metal of the Pisacas. Her body is adorned with a blue necklace and with girdle-strings having (all) the colours in the world (?).

49. Her upper-garment was made in the land of the Abhiras. She shines forth, dreadful, in blue robes. While carrying her metals in wagons and by foot, she is robbed in the woods by blazing thieves.

50. These Horas, whose purpose resides in (the determination of) the thoughts, places of origin, and qualities (of natives), are described by the Greeks by means of illustrations wherein their forms, insignia, and ornaments are successively given. They have names in accordance with their natures.

Select Bibliography

Allen, James P. Genesis in Egypt : The Philosophy of Ancient Egyptian Creation Accounts. New Haven, Conn.: Yale Egyptological Seminar, Dept. of Near Eastern Languages and Civilizations, Graduate School, Yale U, 1988. Print. Yale Egyptological Studies ; 2.

Birch, Samuel. *Records of the past : Being English Translations of the Assyrian and Egyptian Monuments.* London, 1873. Print

Katherine Blouin. "L'acqua Nell'antico Egitto. Vita, Rigenerazione, Incantesimo, Medicamento. (Coll. Egitto Antico)." Revue Historique De Droit Français Et étranger (1922-) 84.2 (2006): 281-83. Web.

Bomhard, Anne-Sophie von (2008) The Naos of the Decades, Oxford Centre of Maritime Archaeology.

Bomhard, Anne-Sophie von (1999) The Egyptian Calendar. A Work for Eternity, (London)

BOYAVAL, B.: Graffite grec de l'Osireion d'Abydos. – in: CdÉ 44 (1969)) No records from this particular oracle but there is a invocation in PGM VII etc

Charles, R. H., and August Dillmann. The Book of Enoch. Oxford: Clarendon, 1893. Print. Chapter 86

Cheak, Aaron. 2013. The Perfect Black: Egypt and Alchemy. In *Alchemical Traditions: From Antiquity to the Avant-Garde.* Edited by Aaron Cheak. Melbourne: Numen Books, pp. 44–91. [**Google Scholar**]

Crum, W. E. Catalogue of the Coptic Manuscripts in the British Museum. London: British Museum, Printed by Order of the Trustees, 1905. Print.

Day, John. God's Conflict with the Dragon and the Sea : Echoes of a Canaanite Myth in the Old Testament. Cambridge: Cambridge UP, 1985. Print. Cambridge Oriental Publications ; No. 35.

Desroches-Noblecourt, Christiane, and F. L. Kenett. *Tutankhamen : Life and Death of a Pharaoh.* London: Penguin, 1989. Print.

de Wit. C. Les inscriptions du temple d'Opet à Karnak I, II, III Bibliotheca Aegyptiaca XI, XII, Bruxelles, 1958, 1962, 196

Doedens, Jaap. The Sons of God in Genesis 6:1-4 : Analysis and History of Exegesis. Leiden ; Boston, 2019. see Douglas Petrovich's review in Oudtestamentische Studiën, Old Testament Studies 76. Web.)

Egypt Exploration Society. The Excavation of the Osireion at Abydos. 1925. Print.

El-Sayed, Rafed, Yahya Masri, and Victoria Altmann-Wendling. Athribis. I, General Site Survey 2003-2007, Archaeological & Conservation Studies : The Gate of Ptolemy IX : Architecture and Inscriptions. Le Caire, 2012. Print. Publications De L'Institut Français D'archéologie Orientale Du Caire ; 1010.

Frankfort, Henri, Adriaan De Buck, and Battiscombe G. Gunn. The Cenotaph of Seti I at Abydos. London], And] ; [Antrim, N. H.: [Sold at the Offices of the Egypt Exploration Society [etc.],], 1933. Print. Memoir (Egypt Exploration Fund) ; 39th.

Frankfurter (1997) in Peter Schäfer; Hans Kippenberg. *Envisioning Magic, A Princeton Seminar and Symposium.* Leiden, Boston, 1997. Numen Book Ser. 75. Web.)

Graham, Lloyd. "Which Seth? Untangling Some Close Homonyms from Ancient Egypt and the Near East." Prague Egyptological Studies 27 (2021): 60–96. Web.

Grimes, Shannon. 2018. *Becoming Gold: Zosimos of Panopolis and the Alchemical Arts in Roman Egypt.* Auckland: Rubedo Press. [**Google Scholar**]

Kemboly, Mpay. The Question of Evil in Ancient Egypt. London: Golden House, 2010. Print.

Egyptology (London, England) ; 12. 376 kem

Lindsay, Jack. The Origins of Alchemy in Graeco-Roman Egypt. London: Muller, 1970. Print.

O'Mara, Patrick F. The Palermo Stone and the Archaic Kings of Egypt. La Canada, Calif: Paulette Pub., 1979. Print. Studies in the Structural Archaeology of Ancient Egypt. Vol 2 p23

Parker, Richard A. (Richard Anthony). The Calendars of Ancient Egypt. Chicago, Illinois: The University of Chicago Press, 1950. Print."

Piankoff, Alexandre. Les Chapelles De Tout-Ankh-Amon. Le Caire: Impr. De L'Institut Français D'archéologie Orientale, 1951. Print. Mémoires Publiés Par Les Membres De L'Institut Français D'archéologie Orientale Du Caire ; T.72.

Pingree, David "The Indian Iconography of the Decans and Horas" *Journal of the Warburg and Courtauld Institutes.* Vol 26, No 3/4 (1963) pp223-254

Reader, Colin. "The Age of the Sphinx and the Development of the Giza Necropolis." In Cooke, Ashley, and Fiona Simpson, eds. Current Research in Egyptology II. Oxford: Archaeopress, 2005, pp. 47-56.

Renouf, P. Le Page, and Edouard Naville. The Egyptian

Book of the Dead : Translation and Commentary. London: Society of Biblical Archaeology, 1904. Print.

Renouf, P. Le Page. Astronomical Observations in the Fifteenth Century before Christ. 1868. Print.

Rinotas, Athanasios. 2021. "Spiritual and Material Conversion in the Alchemical Work of Zosimus of Panopolis" *Religions* 12, no. 11: 1008. https://doi.org/10.3390/rel12111008 (good bibliography)

Roberson, Joshua Aaron. *The Ancient Egyptian Books of the Earth* (2012). Print.

Roberson, Joshua. "An Enigmatic Wall from the Cenotaph of Seti I at Abydos." Journal of the American Research Center in Egypt 43 (2007): 93-112. Web.

Reymond "worship of the ancestor gods at Edfu" Chronique d E 38: 49-70 1963: 68)

Roberts, Alison. 2019. *Hathor's Alchemy: The Ancient Roots of the Hermetic Art*. East Sussex: Northgate Publishers. [**Google Scholar**]

Schoch, Robert M. "How Old Is the Sphinx?". Boston, Massachusetts: Privately Published, 1992. Print.

Tallet, Pierre, and Mark Lehner. The Red Sea Scrolls: How Ancient Papyri Reveal the Secrets of the Pyramids. London, 2021. Print.

Traunecker, C Varia autour du temple d'Opet à Karnak, Pharaon Magazin 41, pp 44-52, 42, pp 8-17

The New Year Procession in the staircase at Edfu and Dendara?

Waddell, W. G. *Manetho*. Cambridge, Mass. : London: Harvard UP ; Heinemann, 2004. Print. Loeb Classical Library ; 350.

West, John Anthony. Serpent in the Sky : The High Wisdom of Ancient Egypt. 1st ed. New York: Harper & Row, 1979. Print.

Index

Symbols

365 lamps 55

A

Abraxas 106
Abydos 43
Acanthus 109
Acheulean 28
Aker 49
Akhmin 47
Alchemy 15, 47, 62, 100, 109
Almagest 56
Alphabet 89
Amduat 75, 103, 104
Angels 17, 20, 28, 31
Ankhew, Akhew, & Neterew 19
Antaeopolis 8, 14
Anubis 11, 26
Apocalypse 71
Apophis 24, 74, 79, 95
Aquifer 48
Asses 7
Atlantis 33, 85, 91
Atum 53
Augustine of Hippo 15
Aza 16
Azael 16

B

Ba'al 59
Babalon 58
Baraka 98
Barbelo 26
Bastard 19
Beginning 5

Belzoni 43
Beresheet 16
Bes 109
Blood 19
Bohak, Gideon 19
Book of Enoch 7, 15, 19, 32, 47, 58
Book of Gates 75
Book of Nwt 48
Building texts 64
Byk 62

C

Cairo 86, 95
    Synagogue Genizah 72
Calendars 56
Canaan 59
Candalas 122
Cardinal 85
Cattle Cult 8
Celestial pole 82
Cenozoic 94
Chaldean 17
Chamber 48
Chaos Kampf, Chaos Struggle, 74
Chaos magick 22
Chronicle 55
City of the Dead 58
Cleopatra 64
Companions 13, 58
Contra Apion 34
Coptic 31, 109
Coptos 72
Cosmogenesis 71
Cow Stone 73
Critias, The 53, 91
Crocodiles 11

D

Dead Sea Scrolls 19
Death 95
    Customs 59
    Posture 75
Decans 80
Decapitated 48
Deep 75
    Mythology 94
Demigods 34, 57, 58
Demonic 103
    Initiator 104
Demons 17, 18, 31
Dendera 11, 55
Dieleman 22
Djeba 85
Djed pillar 78, 79
Djet 78
Djoser 56
Draco 82, 84
Dreaming 109
Drowning 88

E

Earth 5
Earthquakes 92
Edfu 66, 67
Egg 95
Egregori 58
Egypt 33
Elephantine 63, 68
Epilepsy 19
Equinox 80
Esna 24
Essene 19
Essenes 19, 57

Evil 74
Exodus 20, 34
Eye 79

F

Falcon 58, 62
Fayum 8
Fetus 78
Fish 105
Flood 19
Folklore 22
Fries, Jan 22
Funeral
    One's own 70

G

Genesa 72
Geomancy 70
Ghost 94
Giant 8, 17, 20, 100
    Becoming 106
Gibborim 15
Giza 35
Gobekli Tepe 79
Godform 21
God's Wife of Amun 29
Golden Shrine 106
Great White 78
Greek Magical Papyri 22
Gurna 43

H

Harem Conspiracy 61
Hathor 6
Hatshepsut 81
Hawk 85
Head 62, 105
Hebrews 59
Heirlooms 71
Heka 98

Netri 70
Heliopolis 78, 86, 95
Hell 19
Hephaestus 53, 54
Hermeticism 89, 91
Hibis 71
Hiera techne 47
Hierakonpolis 67
Hieroglyphs 6, 85
Hippo 11, 13, 58, 59
    Gorgops 11
Hollow Earth 5
Holocene 73
Horoi 57
Horus 21, 62
    Followers of 58
House of Life 60, 61
Hyksos 34, 59

I

Incubation 29
Initiation 48
International 20
Iron 13
Isden 77, 79
Isis and Osiris 8
Island
    Earth 75
    Of Peace 63
    Of the Trampling 63
Israelites 20

J

Jehovah 59
Jewish chronology 34
Jews 17, 34
Jubilees 23

K

Kamasterion 116

Kemboly, Mpay 74
Khafre 37
Kheops 8
Khoiak 55
Khufu 8, 37, 40
Kingship 54
Knights Templar 16

L

Lakes 76
Land 5
Land of Him who is Great of Arm 76
Lepers 34
Leviathan 79
Library at Alexandria 15
Lilit 18
Lost books 70
Lunar month 56

M

Magical Papyri (PGM) 30
Magick 84
Mandala 85
Manetho 23, 24, 32, 91
    Egyptiaca 34, 51
Mansion of Isden 79
Massey, Gerald 80
Megaliths 68
Memory 61, 83
    Cell of 82
Memphis 54
Mesocosm 82
Metalwork 15, 20
Milky Way 106
Mimesis 98
Min 72
Miniaturization 22
Mizraim 33
Moon 88
Mooring post 80, 82
Moses of Abydos 109

Mounds 70
Mummy 58
   Screaming 61
Musick 70
   Of the spheres 70
Mystery cults 61
Mythology 94

N

Nagada 58
Names 20
Napta playa 72
Necromancy 59
Nectanebo 30
Neith 23, 33, 91
Nephthys 7
Nightmare 19
Nile 88
Noah 88, 92
Nocturnal sun 106
Nummulites 8
Nwt 106, 107

O

Ombos 58
Opening of the Mouth 22, 71
Oracle 34
Orion 92
Osireion 45, 70
Osiris 62, 88
   Tomb of 47
Oxen 7

P

Palermo stone 55
Papyrus Harris 109
Papyrus Salt 61
Pay-lands 76
Pen 79
Persian 17

Petrie 58
Phallus 105
Philo 15
Pillars 51
Place-in-which-the-Enemies-were-
      Annihilated 76
Plato 33
Pleiades 97
Plutarch 30
Polaris 84
Poseidon 92
Positivist 83
Precession 57
Predynastic 36
Primary Corpus 106
Primeval ones 78
Prostitution 29
Ptah 53, 54
Ptolemies 62, 64
Pyramid 9, 35, 49, 107
   Great 55

Q

Queer 59
Qumran 19

R

Rabbinical 17
Read, Jason 22
Reader, Colin 39
Rebels 11
Red 112
Red Sea harbor 40
Renenutet 95
Reproductive Images 78
Resurrection 87
   Chamber 47, 48, 51
Richat Structure 26
Route of the Sungod 103
Ruach Zecharit, the spirit of nightmare
      19

Rush mat 112

S

Sacred Book
   Early Primeval Ones 70
   of the Temples 63
Sages 70, 79
Sahara 26, 72
Sahidic 51
Sai'di 51
Sais 91
Sand 70
Sandal 11
Saqqara 40, 69
Satan 32
Satet 63, 68
Schoch, Robert 39
Scientology 83
Scribes 25, 98
Sekhmet 113
Semjâzâ
   Enchantments, and root-cuttings 20
Senenmut 80, 81, 82
Senwosret 53
Serapis 110
Seriadic land 51
Serpent 78
   Nest 95
Seth 7, 8, 21, 26, 48
   And the Two Ways 74
   Black Bones of 8
Seth-Typhon 59
Sethites 19, 26
Seven 97
   Builders 77
   Sages 77, 97
Sexual 106
Shabaka 54
   Stone 54, 60
Shale 48
Shamanic 22

Shebtiw 23, 74, 75, 82
Sheshat 77, 87
Shu 54, 90, 95
Shunet el-Zebib 68
Sirius 55
Skemiophris 54
Smaout en Set 58
Snake 32
Sobek 92
Sobekneferu 54
Sokar 49
Solon 91
Solstice 80
Solve and coagula 106
Sons of God 28
Spells 76
Sphinx 35
Spirits of the Dead 34, 58, 59
Star Maps 80
Strabo 29
Submerged 83
Sun and moon 106
Superman 17
Syncellus 51, 56

T

Tallet 41
Tamarisk 100
Tanen 85
Tankhem 40

Temenos 100, 103, 113
Ten 77
Tent shrines 66
Territory of the Ancestor 76
Theatre 61
Theosebeia 47
Thinis 53
Third synthetic class of being 19
Thoth 33, 51, 70, 77
Thuban 84
Tiamat 79
Timaeus 91
Toponyms 11
Troublesome 21
Tura 40
Turin 68
    King list 54
Tutankhamun 11, 47
Two Brothers 26
    Myth of the 26
Typhon 8, 95
Typhonians 59, 75, 109

U

Umm el Qaab 47
Underworld 75
    of the soul 70, 95
Ursa major 97

V

Vatican 78
Virgo 57
Voteresses 29

W

War in heaven 80
Waset 43
Watchers 15, 19, 58, 97
Water damage 39
West, John Anthony
    Serpent and the Sky 37
Whales 8
Witchblood 19

Y

Yamm 92

Z

Zodiac 58
Zohar 16, 84
Zosimus 20, 47, 109
    Book of Pictures 47

9 781914 153273